W9-CBD-336

WORD STUDIES

ON THE

HOLY SPIRIT

by

E.W. Bullinger

Foreword by Warren W. Wiersbe

KREGEL PUBLICATIONS
Grand Rapids, Michigan 49501

Word Studies on the Holy Spirit, by E. W. Bullinger. Foreword by Warren W. Wiersbe. Copyright © 1979 by Kregel Publications, a division of Kregel, Inc. P. O. Box 2607, Grand Rapids, MI, 49501. All rights reserved. (Previously titled *The Giver and His Gifts*.) First paperback edition published in 1985.

Library of Congress Cataloging-in-Publication Data

Bullinger, E. W. (Ethelbert William), 1837–1913.
  Word Studies on the Holy Spirit.

  Originally published: The Giver and His Gifts.
London: Eyre & Spottiswoode, 1905.

  Includes indexes.

  1. Pneuma (The Greek word) 2. Holy Spirit – Biblical
teaching. 3. Bible. N.T. – Criticism, interpretation, etc.
4. Soul – Terminology. 5. Spirit – Terminology. I. Title
PA878.P5B8   1985   231.'3   85-7631

ISBN   0-8254-2246-9 (pb)

  4 5 6 7 Printing/Year 93 92 91 90

Printed in the United States of America

WORD STUDIES
ON THE
HOLY SPIRIT

Contents

Foreword

The emphasis in recent years on the doctrine of the Holy Spirit has helped to produce a great number of books on that subject. Some of these books are immature and will not last. Their theology (to borrow a phrase from P.T. Forsyth) is "like a bad photograph — over-exposed and under-developed." But a few books have made a definite contribution to the subject and will surely last.

Word Studies on the Holy Spirit is one of the older works that has had a steady ministry and is sure to last. For one thing, the author was in his day widely accepted as a scholar in Biblical languages and textual criticism. Even those who disagreed with Dr. Bullinger's conclusions had to admit that he was an "indefatigable Bible scholar."

This book is unique in that it is both a concordance and a concise commentary on every verse in the New Testament that uses the word "spirit" (*pneuma*). It enables the serious student of the Word to examine each reference and compare Scripture with Scripture. Is there any better way to discern the mind of the Lord on a given subject?

To be sure, the author introduces some of his own special interpretations, particularly with reference to Israel and the Church. We may not agree with him, but at least we have the opportunity to examine our own convictions in the light of his thinking. It has been well said that he who knows only his own position does not know even that. It is good to widen our outlook even if we do not change our position; for, as Dorothy Sayers wrote: "There's nothing you can't prove if your outlook is only sufficiently limited."

Ethelbert William Bullinger was born on December 15, 1837, in Canterbury, England, a direct descendant of the great Swiss Reformer, Johann Heinrich Bullinger. He was a choirboy at Canterbury Cathedral and studied music with some of the leading men of his day. However, it was serious Bible study that captured his interest. He trained for the Anglican Church ministry at King's College, London and while there showed skill in Biblical languages. The Archbishop of Canterbury recognized this skill by granting Bullinger an honorary Doctor of Divinity degree in 1881.

Bullinger's studies convinced him that traditional doctrines concerning Israel and the Church were wrong, so he began an independent ministry of the Word. He founded *Things to Come,* a Bible study magazine that presented his dispensational views. He authored a number of books that are unique in their fields, such as *The Witness of the Stars, Number in Scripture,* and *The Critical Lexicon and Concordance to the English and Greek New Testaments.* His greatest work, *The Companion Bible,* contains the results of his life-time of tireless searching of the Scriptures.

He died in London on June 6, 1913. Most people remember him only for his beautiful tune for Frances Ridley Havergal's hymn, "I am trusting Thee, Lord Jesus." Serious students of the Bible remember him as one who dared to search into God's truth and follow it wherever it led him. We may not agree with all that Dr. Bullinger has written, but we must confess that he stimulates us to give our very best to the study of the Word of God.

September 1979   WARREN W. WIERSBE

Introduction

WE are familiar with the word "Christology": which is applied to a study of such passages of God's Word as speak of "Christ" both by way of evidence, and of doctrine.

In the same way we may use the word "*Pneumatology*": as describing a study of all the passages which refer to *pneuma*, or spirit.

There are works bearing on the subject of "Psychology," and treating of passages which refer to ψυχή (*psyche*) *life* or *soul*. Also on the subject of "Physiology," which has to do with man's *nature* as a whole: and is used of man as a complex being, with special reference to the body.

But there is yet room for a work which shall deal specially with the word *pneuma*.

There has been much written on the subject of the Holy Spirit, both as to Himself and His work: but something is needed which shall embrace a wider field of enquiry and study. The word *pneuma*, both in its use and usage, requires more careful and systematic examination than it has yet received. And in this larger range the subject might appropriately be called "Pneumatology."

1

Few subjects are of greater importance, or fraught with weightier consequences to our theology, than this : which bears directly upon the Holy Spirit, and upon His operations in connection with the Church of God as a whole, and with the individual experience of the child of God.

And yet there are few subjects which have received less attention and study; and few about which there are greater differences of opinion among Christians.

In *The Expository Times* for May, 1903, the editor commences a review of a certain book with these words :—

"The doctrine of the Holy Spirit still suffers neglect among us. Spasmodically we beat our breasts, and say, ' Go to, we must preach the Holy Ghost ! But the people do not understand. We ourselves do not understand.' "

This confession, coupled with the number of letters which we constantly receive enquiring as to the meaning and teaching of certain passages (such, especially, as 2 Cor. iii. 6, 17, 18. Eph. v. 18. John iii. 5 ; iv. 21-24. Acts xix. 2, &c.), points to the necessity of some exhaustive treatment of this subject.

The question we have to ask, and the information we seek, is this : To what does the word *pneuma* refer each time it is used in the New Testament ? When does it refer to the Holy Spirit ? And when is it used psychologically or in any other way ? In other words, when ought *pneuma* to be rendered Spirit, and when spirit ? When with a capital "S," and when with a small " s " ?

The answer is, that we can get no help, either from the original Greek manuscripts, the Printed Greek Texts, the Authorised Version, or the Revised Version.

Hence the necessity of our present effort : so that our readers may be able to answer these questions for themselves.

1. We can get no help from the ORIGINAL GREEK MANUSCRIPTS of the New Testament.

There are nearly four thousand of them ; but they are all in one of two styles of writing.

The one class is written all in capitals without any small letters. The other class is written all in small letters with no capitals, or with only a very few ; none as we use them, with certain words ; but only at the beginning of books or sections, or of large paragraphs.

The former class consists of about 127 manuscripts, called " Uncials "[1] because every letter is large, and the whole is written in capitals.

The other class consists of about 3,702 manuscripts, which are called " Cursives "[2] because every word is written in *running-hand*.

It is clear, therefore, that we can get no help from the manuscripts as to when to use " S," and when to use " s."

2. We can get no help from the PRINTED EDITIONS of the GREEK TESTAMENT.

The MSS. have been printed at different times by various scholars, who have edited particular editions.[3] The most important are as follows :—

> The Complutensian Polyglot[4]   1514
> Erasmus (1st Edition)[5]   ...   1516

---

[1] So called from the late Latin *uncia, an inch*, from the large size of the letters.

[2] From the Latin *cursivus, flowing* ; hence, of hand-writing, *running*, or as we say, " running-hand " from *currere, to run*.

[3] These Editions, where quoted, are indicated by their initial letter.

[4] Though prepared by this date, the printing was delayed till 1522. So that Erasmus's first edition is known as the earliest printed Greek Testament.

[5] The subsequent Editions were published in 1519, 1522, 1527, 1535.

Stephens[1]	...	...	...	1546-49
Beza[2] ...	...	...	...	1566
Elzevir[3]	...	...	...	1624
Griesbach	...	...	...	1774-75
Scholz ...	...	...	...	1830-36
Lachmann	...	...	...	1831-50
Tischendorf	...	...	...	1841-72
Tregelles	...	...	...	1856-72
Alford ...	...	...	...	1862-71
Wordsworth	...	...	...	1870
The Revisers' Text	...	...	1881
Westcott & Hort	...	...	1881-1903.

There are other less known editions, such as the recent edition by the late Dr. Weymouth, and Dr. Scrivener.[4]

These editors *all differ among themselves* as to the use of capital letters. They have used them according to their best judgment, of course; but still it is their own judgment, and is, therefore, a matter of interpretation rather than of *transcription*.

The same may be said of their paragraphs, parentheses, inverted commas, punctuation, etc. These, with chapters, verses, head-lines, etc., are all editorial, and rest only on human authority.

It is clear, therefore, that we can get no help from the printed texts of the Greek Testament.

3. We can get little or no help from the English AUTHORISED VERSION of 1611.

Since the original edition of the A.V., in 1611, many

---

[1] This Version (as well as the Elzevir) is spoken of as the *Textus Receptus;* or Received Text. In the main they are the same.

[2] Subsequent Editions of Beza were printed in 1582, 1589, 1598.

[3] This is also spoken of sometimes as the Received Text.

[4] This last, published by Bell & Co., is the best for general use, as it consists of the " Received Text," with every "various reading " printed in thick type, and the Editorial Authorities for and against them.

editions have been printed by the three great presses (Oxford, Cambridge and London); and, in these, great modifications have been made, and changes have been introduced from time to time, especially in the Cambridge editions of 1629 and 1638. More systematic revisions were made by Dr. Paris in the Cambridge edition of 1762, and by Dr. Blayney in the Oxford edition of 1769. These included the use of italic type, references, headings, chronology, capital letters, etc. But, as the Revisers say in their Preface, "none of them, however, rest on any higher authority than that of the persons who from time to time superintended the publication."

We may further say that none of the current editions of the A.V. exactly represents that of 1611.

This is specially true as to the use of capital letters.

In many cases where that had a "s" for spirit (or "g" for ghost) the current editions have "S" and "G." And the opposite is also the case; in several passages where the 1611 edition had "S," the current editions, to-day, have "s."[1]

Thus the Authorised Version is no help to us in this matter.

The use of capital letters was much more common in the seventeenth century than at the present day; such words as Altar, Ark, Court, Mercy-seat, Priest, Sabbath, etc., always had capitals. In later times the tendency has been to diminish their use: but, strange to say, while this has been the case with all other nouns, the change has been in the opposite direction with regard to the word "spirit." The small "s" of 1611 has in very many cases been replaced by a large "S" in the subsequent Editions. This is the more to be regretted, because, whether other nouns have capital letters or not does not

---

[1] All these changes and differences are noted in our complete list of passages which follows.

affect the sense of the passage. But with the word "spirit" the case is quite different. With this word the use of the capital letter becomes at once a case of *interpretation* rather than of mere *translation*.

As our aim is to obtain the Divine interpretation of the word *pneuma*, we shall have to discard the *interpretation* thus given to us by the Translators, and irresponsible Editors of the A.V.

We have noted in all cases their use of small and capital letters in each passage; together with the changes from the edition of 1611; so that all the data may be in the hands of our readers.

4. We can get no help from the REVISED VERSION of 1881.

The Revisers make no reference to the use of capital letters in their preface. But a very slight examination will show that, whereas they have greatly diminished the use of capital letters for ordinary nouns, they have greatly increased the use of "S" in the word "spirit," and of "G" in the word "ghost."

This may be easily seen in the several "parallel" editions, where the text of 1611 is given side by side with the Revisers' edition of 1881.

It is clear, therefore, that we can get no help from the Revised Version.

It is a question whether there be two versions in any language which are absolutely uniform in their use of the letters " S " and " s."

The translators themselves have no guide beyond that afforded by the presence or absence of the definite article, and by the context. Aided by these they can express only their own opinion and give only their own *interpretation*.

No two of them being alike, not one of them can be taken as a standard or as a guide.

The Bible student is, therefore, thrown back on his own

resources: and he can find the truth only by examining each one of the many occurrences of the word; and form his own conclusions and his judgment by the manner in which the Divine Author of the Word of God has used it.

The *use* depends on a knowledge of the original; and the *usage* depends on a knowledge of all the contexts.

The two together will hardly ever fail to lead to a correct understanding of any or all of the passages where the word occurs.

To show the importance of the whole subject; and, to calm the minds of any who may feel that we are unnecessarily raising disturbing questions, it may be sufficient to show that we are not the first, or the only ones, who have realised the difficulty, if we quote the words of the late J. N. Darby, in the Preface to the second edition of his translation of the New Testament (1884). He says:—

" The use of a large or small ' s ' is of extreme difficulty in the case of the word Spirit; not in giving it when the Holy Spirit is simply spoken of personally. There it is simple enough. But as dwelling in us, our state by it, and the Holy Spirit itself, are so blended as to make it then very difficult; because it is spoken of as our state, and then as the Holy Ghost. If it be put large, we lose the first; if small, the Spirit personally. I can only leave it with this warning, calling the attention of the reader to it. It is a blessed thought that it is so blended in power that our state is so spoken of; but if we lose the divine Person, that blessing itself is lost. The reader may see, not the difficulty, for it does not exist there, but the blending of the effect and the person in Rom. viii. 27."

On Rom. viii. 9, he has this note, " Another instance of the difficulty of putting a large or small ' s.' It is clearly the state and characteristic of the believer; but it is so by the presence of the Spirit."

Here then we have the difficulty stated and acknowledged. And we ask, What advance has been made in the solution of this "difficulty" in the twenty years that have elapsed since these words were written by Mr. Darby?

Have his successors done anything to remove the difficulty? Have they not, instead of advancing in the knowledge of the Scriptures, settled down "on their lees," as though their leaders had exhausted the treasures of the inexhaustible Word?

Our desire is, therefore, to put the English reader in possession of all the facts of the case; so that he may be independent of all human teachers.

We propose (1) to show every way in which *use* is made of the words "spirit" and "holy," in all their various combinations.

(2) To give a classified list of every *usage*; *i.e.*, every sense in which the words are employed, in Scripture, both jointly, and severally; whether with or without the article.

(3) To add a complete list of all the passages where the words occur; giving each in full, pointing out the particular words employed (the *use*); with notes sufficient to show and explain the particular *usage* in each case.

In this way light will be shed on many important and difficult scriptures; mistakes will be explained, errors corrected, and truth, which has been obscured, again recovered from the inspired Word.

The word πνεῦμα *(pneuma)*, *spirit*, occurs 385 times in the Greek Received Text. Of these, the Critical Texts of Griesbach, Lachmann, Tischendorf, Tregelles, Alford, and the Revisers, agree in omitting nine* and in adding

---

* These nine passages are Luke ii. 40; ix. 55. Acts xviii. 5. Romans viii. 1. 1 Cor. vi. 20. Eph. v. 9. 1 Tim. iv. 12. 1 Peter i. 22. 1 John v. 7.

three.† These twelve passages will all be pointed out as we come to them in their respective places, where we shall note the changes involved.

There are, therefore, in all, 388 passages to be dealt with, affecting the use and usage of *pneuma*.

The word is thus distributed in the New Testament.

Books	Gross Total	To be Omitted *	To be Added †	Net Total
The Gospels	105	2	—	103
The Acts	69	—	1	70
The Church Epistles ...	140	4	1	137
Paul's other Epistles ...	21	1	—	20
General Epistles ...	27	2	—	25
Apocalypse	23	—	1	24
	385	9	3	379

In these 385 passages of the Received Text, the word *pneuma* is rendered in the current editions of the A.V. as follows :

Renderings		*Times*	Totals
Spirit ...	...	133	
spirit ...	...	153	
spiritual	...	1	
ghost ...	...	2	
life	...	1	
wind ...	...	1	291

With the Genitive case

spiritually	...	—	1

With hagion

Holy Spirit ...	4	
Holy Ghost ...	89	93
		385

† These three passages are Acts iv. 25. Phil. iv. 23. Rev. xxii. 6.

In the margin, *breath* is twice given as an alternative rendering (once for spirit and once for life). *Of the spirit* (for spiritually), once; and, *spirit* (for spiritual) once.

All these facts, taken together, show the necessity for some further study of this great and important subject.

The Use of *Pneuma* in the New Testament

Let us next note the various ways in which the Greek word πνεῦμα, *pneuma*, is employed: *i.e.*, the way in which it is *used* (apart from its meanings, or the sense which is given to it: *i.e.*, its *usage*):—

i. It is used alone, in two ways

> (1) without the article: simply πνεῦμα (*pneuma*).
>
> (2) with the article: τὸ πνεῦμα (*to pneuma*) *the pneuma*.

ii. It is employed with ἅγιον (*hagion*) *holy*, in four ways:

> (1) *pneuma hagion* (holy spirit) Matt. i. 18, and in 49 other places.
>
> (2) *hagion pneuma* (spirit holy) 1 Cor. vi. 19, etc.
>
> (3) *the hagion pneuma*, Matt. xxviii. 19, etc.
>
> (4) *the pneuma the hagion*, Matt. xii. 32, etc.

iii. It is used with *pronouns: e.g., the pneuma of me: i.e.*, my *pneuma*, Matt. xii. 18, etc.

iv. It is used with *prepositions*, which affect its sense:

> (1) ἐν πνεύματι (*en pneumati*), by or through the Spirit: denoting agency.
>
> (2) Adverbially, as meaning spiritually and sometimes (like ἐν δόλῳ, (*en dolō*), craftily, 2 Cor. xii. 16): thus turning the phrase into an *adverb*.

v. It is employed in combination with the Divine Names in seven different forms; of which four have the article, and three are without: *e.g., pneuma Theou; pneuma Christou*, etc.

vi. It is employed with ten other nouns in the genitive
case, which (by *Enallage*) qualify the meaning
of *pneuma*. These again are used with and
without the article: *e.g.*, a *pneuma* of sonship
(Rom. viii. 15), *i.e.*, a sonship-*pneuma*.

vii. It is employed with a second noun with which it
is joined by a conjunction (*Hendiadys*). Thus
used it becomes a superlative adjective.

Here are seven different ways in which the word
pneuma is employed. Each class is distinct, to say
nothing of the minor variations.

Now, the question is, are we to make no difference in
our reading and understanding of these various uses?
Can it be that God employs the word *pneuma* in all
these different ways, and yet has no object in so doing
and has only one meaning for them all?

Surely, no one will contend that this is the case.
Judging by the perfection of all God's other works, we
know that His *Word* and His *words* are alike perfect.
He not only means what He says, but He has a meaning for everything He says. If He uses one word, there
is a reason why no other word would do. If He uses
this word in several distinct ways, then there must be
a reason for His so doing.

"The words of Jehovah are pure words:
 As silver tried in a furnace.
 [Words] pertaining to the earth,
 But purified seven times" (Ps. xii. 6).

His way is perfect . . . His word is refined (Ps. xviii.
30, marg.).

The *words* of which the *Word* is made up are perfect
in themselves, perfect in their use, perfect in their order,
and perfect in their truths.

If God has given a revelation in writing, then it must
be in words, and the words must be His words. There-

fore they must be inspired. They may be spoken by human lips, and written by human hands, but He calls them " His words." Whatever human agency or instrumentality may be employed, it is still His act. Hence we read " this scripture must needs be fulfilled, which the Holy Ghost by the mouth of David spake before concerning Judas " (Acts i. 16). David's lips uttered them; David's pen wrote them down; but they were not David's words. They were the words " which the Holy Ghost spake." It was He who spake them. We cannot get beyond this, if we would seek a definition of Inspiration. All theories are useless in the face of this statement of fact: (compare Acts iii. 18. Heb. i. 1. 2 Peter i. 21).

Whatever the difference may be, therefore, in the various uses of the word *pneuma*, we may be certain that there is a Divinely perfect reason for such use in each case ; and it is our great business to search it out.

The works of the LORD are great,

Sought out of all them that have pleasure therein

(Ps. cxii. 2).

His Word is the greatest of His works; and His words, therefore, are to be sought out by all who, through grace, have been made to value them more than their necessary food.

If we confound that which God has carefully distinguished, we must of necessity be landed in hopeless confusion ; and all doctrine based on that confusion must itself be confused, and can only mislead.

If God has made a difference in His employment of the word *pneuma*, we cannot ignore that difference without serious loss.

Our business must be to read, mark, and study what He has written for our learning.

The Usage of *Pneuma* in the New Testament

Let us next observe the USAGE; that is to say, the various senses in which God has employed this word *pneuma*. We have seen its *use*, *i.e.*, the various ways in which He has employed it; we have now to see its *usage*; *i.e.*, the various *meanings* which He has given it.

No Lexicons, or other works or words of man can avail us here. It is only from God's own Word that we can learn His truths. It is only by carefully observing what He has said, and how He has said it; what words He has used, and how He has used them; that we can discover the meaning which we are to put upon what He has written for our learning. Only thus can we understand His word.

As to the *usage* of the word (as distinct from its *use*) we note:

I. The word *pneuma* is used of GOD Himself or the "Father." "God is *pneuma*" (John iv. 24). It is His Divine Nature that is spoken of. The statement is simplicity itself. "God is *pneuma*."

II. The word *pneuma* is used of CHRIST, the second Person of the Trinity. He, in resurrection, became a quickening or life-giving *pneuma* (1 Cor. xv. 45). He became "living soul" in Incarnation; but "life-giving *pneuma*" in Resurrection. What this is in itself, and what it is in relation to the Resurrection body, we shall see under 1 Cor. xv. 45 below, in the list of passages. Compare *usage* No. xii. There are other passages where Christ is spoken of as *pneuma*, but these we must consider in their own place and order in the complete list of all the occurrences of *pneuma*, which follows. (We may refer especially to 2 Cor. iii. 6, 17, 18.)

III. It is used of the HOLY SPIRIT. Because He is emphatically the Spirit of God, the great mistake has been made of concluding, without sufficient thought or care, that the word *pneuma* must nearly always refer to Him, wherever it may be used.

This mistake is so general that, even where there is no article in the Greek, the definite article is often introduced and imported into the English ; and where there is nothing to indicate capital letters in the original, they have been used without any Textual authority in the English and other translations.

This practice has been the fruitful source of many very popular errors. The English reader has been helpless in this matter. He sees the definite article, and the capital letters, in the English, and naturally concludes that " the Holy Spirit " is meant. He does not know that he is reading an interpretation or comment, instead of what ought to be a simple translation. He takes it as Divine and inspired ; and proceeds to reason on these expressions, to draw his inferences, to form his views, and to build up his schemes of doctrine and teaching upon them. But his theories are based on a human foundation ; his doctrines are built, not on the impregnable rock of the Divine words, but on the opinions and judgment of man.

In this lies the secret of many mistakes in the teaching of the present day. And here, too, lies the importance of our present course of study.

When it is presently seen that there are no less than fourteen distinct *usages* of the word *pneuma* (besides the several ways in which the word is *used*), the need of our investigation will be at once recognised.

We have to discover, when the Holy Spirit is meant ;

or when some other meaning is to be given to the word *pneuma*.

The use of the definite article is most important as a guide to help us in the formation of our judgment ; but the context is a still more important guide.   The two together will seldom leave us in doubt as to what is the exact meaning to be given to the word, and when the Holy Spirit is meant : *e.g.* :

In Acts v. 3, we read " why hath Satan filled thine heart to lie to *the pneuma the holy* ? " *i.e.*, the Holy Spirit.

In Acts xiii. 2, " *The pneuma the holy* said."

In Acts xv. 28, " It seemed good to *the holy pneuma** and to us."

In Acts xxviii. 25, " Well spake *the pneuma the holy* by Isaiah the prophet."

This full expression is not always necessary to denote the Holy Spirit.   The briefer expression is sometimes used ; see Acts xvi. 6, " They were forbidden by *the holy pneuma* to preach the word in Asia."

Here, it means the Holy Spirit, although the expression is not the usual one employed in this connection.

IV. *Pneuma* is used (by *Metonymy*) for the OPERATIONS produced by The Holy Spirit.   " That which is born of *the Pneuma* is *pneuma* " (John iii. 6).   Here in one verse we have two distinct usages of *pneuma*.   First we have the Divine Nature ; and then we have that which is born of or produced by (*ἐκ*) it : *i.e.*, His operations and gifts, which are called *pneuma*.   In 1 Cor. xiv. 12, we read of those who are " zealous of spiritual *gifts* " (margin " Gr. *of spirits* ").   Here the word " gifts " is actually (and rightly) supplied, in italic type (in both

---

* Tisch.   Tregelles, Westcott and Hort, read *the pneuma the holy*, as in ch. v. 3.

versions) ; and the Greek " zealous of spirits " is translated, "zealous of spiritual gifts." This is perfectly
correct.   But it proves to us that we have, here, a
fourth usage of the word *pneuma.*

What these various spiritual works and operations
and gifts are, we are told in 1 Cor. xii. 7-11.*

V.   *Pneuma* is used of the greatest of His spiritual
gifts : for, the NEW NATURE is called *pneuma*.   This is a
special sense found only in the Church Epistles.   This
Pauline sense is quite distinct from the usage of the
word in the Acts of the Apostles.   The New Nature is
the direct result of the operation of the Holy Spirit, and
therefore, according to John iii. 6, it is " spirit," and is
called *pneuma*.   One who possesses this new nature is
said to be "begotten of God."   This *pneuma*, being
Divine, is " perfect," and " doth not commit sin "
(1 John iii. 9; v. 18).   The Old Nature (which in contra-
distinction from " spirit ") is called " flesh," cannot but
sin (Rom. viii. 7).   It is " enmity against God.   It is not
subject to the law of God, neither indeed can it be."

So that the true child of God has these two natures
within him.   They are contrary the one to the other, so
that he often cannot do the good his New Nature would

---

* Indeed, in this chapter (1 Cor. xii.) we have a wonderful revelation as to the Body of Christ—the Mystery or Secret of God.

A | 1-11. *Nine* Spiritual Gifts which God has given to His
　　| Church : (word of wisdom, word of knowledge, faith, gifts of
　　| healing, miracles, prophecy, discerning of spirits, tongues,
　　| interpretations).

　　　　B | 12-17.   The one Body.   Enumeration of members
　　　　　 | (*eight*) : (Jew, Gentile, bond, free : foot, hand, ear,
　　　　　 | eye).

　　　　B | 18-27.   The one Body.   Enumeration of members
　　　　　 | (*eight*) set in the Body (eye, hand, head, feet : feeble
　　　　　 | honourable, uncomely, comely).

A | 28-31. *Nine* Spiritual Gifts which God has given to His
　　| Church : (Apostles, Prophets, Teachers, Miracles, Healings,
　　| Helps, Governments, Tongues, Interpretations).

ever do ; nor, thank God, can he often do the evil, which his Old Nature would ever do.

This conflict must continue so long as we are in this mortal body, because it is equally true " that which is born of the flesh is flesh," and remains flesh, while " that which is born of the Spirit is spirit," and remains spirit (John iii. 6). Flesh is never changed into spirit, and spirit is never changed into flesh. There is no such thing as a " change of heart," of which so many speak. That will be seen one day in the case of Israel (Ezek. xxxvi. 24-29); but not now in the child of God. The presence of this New Nature necessitates conflict with the Old Nature : and this conflict is therefore the best *assurance* that we are "in Christ" (2 Cor. v. 17). This it is which ever distinguishes the true child of God from the mere professor. The true believer always has *an abiding sense of inward corruption ;* while the merely religious person never has it at all, and knows nothing of it.

This New nature is called "*pneuma* ": and the possessors of it walk "according to *pneuma*," and not "according to flesh" (Rom. viii. 4): *i.e.*, with the (spiritual) " mind " the believer " serves the law of God ; and with the flesh the law of sin " (Rom. vii. 25).

A man may *say* he has "no sin ": but he only deceives himself (1 John i. 8): he does not deceive others.

There are other special terms for *Pneuma*, when used of the New Nature. It is called " *pneuma Theou* "; *i.e.*, God's *pneuma*, or Divine spirit (for we are made " partakers of the Divine nature " (2 Pet. i. 4). It is called (the) "*pneuma* of God "; because God is the Creator of it. It is called also "*pneuma Christou* " or " Christ's *pneuma* ": because it is in virtue of this New Nature that we are regarded as being made the " sons of God," even as Christ was " the Son of God " (Rom. viii. 14). As possessors of (the) "*pneuma* of Christ," we are looked at as being children of God, heirs, and joint-heirs with Christ (Rom. viii. 17). Hence it is spoken of as a "sonship-*pneuma*" in verse 15.

Only those who are made, by Divine power, to partake of this *pneuma Theou*, or Divine nature, can possess this New Nature. This at once disposes of all the modern teaching that every man possesses this in himself by natural generation. We see how Divine Truth cuts at the root of all such false teaching, and are shown how the true believer is "God's workmanship, created in Christ Jesus unto good works, which God hath before ordained that we should walk in them" (Eph. ii. 10).

Oh, to be the subjects of His marvellous grace and power! How wonderful! "His workmanship"! And this workmanship forms within us a "new spirit"—a "new nature."

VI. *Pneuma* is used *psychologically* of man's NATURE according to Gen. ii. 7.* By the union of "body" and "*pneuma*," man becomes "living soul," *i.e.*, a living being. When the body returns to dust "as it was" (Gen. iii. 19), and the *pneuma* returns "to God who gave it" (Ecc. xii. 7. Ps. civ. 29, 30), man becomes, and is called, a "dead soul." See Lev. xxi. 11. Num. vi. 6, where the Hebrew "dead *nephesh*" (*soul*), is actually rendered "dead body"! (so as to agree with tradition). And compare Num. ix. 6, 7, 10; xix. 11, 13. It is also used of "the dead" in Lev. xxii. 4. Hag. ii. 13.

Hence, at death the *pneuma* is "commended" to God for His keeping (Ps. xxxi. 5. Luke xxiii. 46. Acts vii. 59), until it shall be re-united with the body in resurrection. While man thus possesses *pneuma*, he is never

---

* Hence, in Jas. iv. 5 it is actually used, by *Metonymy*, for *the old nature*.

once called "*a pneuma*," as angels are. They are *spiritual* beings, man is a *human* being.

All persons have *pneuma*, psychologically : but not all have Divine *pneuma*. In this respect, men are higher, by nature, than animals ; and some men are higher than other men.

VII. *Pneuma* is used of CHARACTER : *e.g.*, we read of "a *pneuma* of cowardice " (2 Tim. i. 7) : *i.e.*, a cowardly spirit : " a *pneuma* of meekness " (1 Cor. iv. 21) : *i.e.*, a meek spirit. The Saviour speaks of those who are " poor as to *the* (or, in their) *pneuma*" : *i.e.*, who are humble and meek (Matt. v. 3). In Rom. viii. 15 we have "a *pneuma* of bondage " (a bond-servant spirit) : " a *pneuma* of sonship " (a sonship-spirit).

VIII. *Pneuma* is used by *Metonymy* of the FEELINGS ; *i.e.*, *the will*, or *mind*, or *desire* of man, because it is *invisible* ; in contrast to the flesh, which is *visible* : *e.g.*, " The *pneuma* is willing, but the flesh is weak " (Matt. xxvi. 41). This cannot, of course, have any of the meanings already considered : the revelation of " the new creation in Christ Jesus," and the gift of the new nature, not having then been made.

IX. *Pneuma* is used, by *Synecdoche*, for THE WHOLE PERSON, or the man himself ; a part being put for the whole. In these cases " my spirit " means *myself*, as " my soul " means *myself* (Luke i. 47). In Mark ii. 8 we read " Jesus perceived in his *pneuma* " ; *i.e.*, *in himself*. In Mark v. 30 we have exactly the same meaning expressed plainly, without a Figure. "And Jesus . . . knowing in himself " (ἐν ἑαυτῷ, *en heautō*). Compare John vi. 61.

[" Flesh " is used in like manner for the person himself in Rom. iii. 20. 1 Cor. i. 29, etc.]

X. *Pneuma* is used also ADVERBIALLY. Either in the simple *Dative* case, or with a preposition : *e.g.*, ἐν δόλῳ (*en dolō*) *craftily*, 2 Cor. xii. 16 : ἐν τάχει (*en tachei*) *speedily*, Rev. i. 1 (not *shortly* as to time, when : but *speedily* as to pace, when once the things begin to come to pass) : ἐν δυνάμει (*en dunamei*) *powerfully*, Rom. i. 4 (which see) : ἐν κρυπτῷ (*en kruptō*) *inwardly, in the hidden parts* (as opposed to outwardly and formally, Rom. ii. 29) or *secretly* (John xviii. 20) : ἐν ἀφροσύνῃ (*en aphrosunē*) *foolishly* (2 Cor. xi. 17).

Thus ἐν πνεύματι (*en pneumati*) may sometimes mean *spiritually* : *i.e.*, *in a spiritual manner* (and may not necessarily imply instrumental agency, as in Ezek. viii. 3 or Rev. i. 10, *by (the) Spirit*) ; though both senses may be true ; for, if done by the instrumentality of the Holy Spirit, it is necessarily done in a spiritual manner.

This usage, therefore, comes to mean *spiritually* in the sense of *essentially, really, and truly* : and implies that what is possessed or done, is so, in the highest degree, in the strongest form, or in the greatest measure.

" Fervent in spirit" means *spiritually fervent*, or exceedingly fervent, or zealous (See Rom. xii. 11. Acts xviii. 25).

That this is a distinct usage is clear, otherwise the Holy Spirit contradicts Himself. In Acts xxi. 4 He said by certain disciples that Paul "should not go up to Jerusalem."

But, in xix. 21, we read that " Paul purposed in the spirit." If this means the Holy Spirit, then the purpose here was contrary to the purpose as expressed in xx. 23 and xxi. 4, 11.

But it means that Paul was *strongly purposed*, that he was *firmly determined* to go. This agrees with xx. 22, " and now behold I go *exceedingly bound*, or impelled, unto Jerusalem."

But it was Paul's own determination in opposition to the warning of the Holy Spirit. " He would not be persuaded " (Acts xxi. 14). Then the Holy Spirit (as distinguished from Paul's *pneuma*) witnessed against him in every city, that bonds and afflictions awaited him in Jerusalem (Acts xx. 23; xxi. 11).

A comparison of Acts xx. 22 with verse 23, establishes this usage.

We meet with it again in Rom. i. 9, "God is my witness, whom I serve with (R.V., in) my *pneuma*": *i.e.*, whom I *zealously* or *diligently serve*.

XI. *Pneuma* is used of ANGELS, or spirit-beings. Thus used, Angels are distinct from *human*-beings, or "flesh and blood" (1 Cor. xv. 50); and distinct also from a human body in resurrection, which has "flesh and bones" (Luke xxiv. 39), and is not therefore truly an angel or spirit-being. · Those, therefore, utter a vain desire who are taught to sing "I want to be an angel." They "want" that which can never "be."

This usage of the word is proved by Heb. i. 7, "he maketh his angels *pneumata*," and Heb. i. 14, "are they not all ministering (or worshipping) *pneumata* sent forth to minister (R.V., do service) for them who shall be heirs of salvation."

Acts viii. 29 and Rev. i. 4 are other examples of this usage. See them in the list to follow.

XII. *Pneuma* is used also of EVIL ANGELS. 1 Tim. iv. 1, "The Spirit (*i.e.*, the Holy Spirit) speaketh expressly, that, in the latter times, some shall depart from the faith, giving heed to seducing (*i.e.*, deceiving or misleading) *pneumata*, and doctrines (*i.e.*, teachings) of demons."

Evil angels are thus distinguished from "demons." But yet demons, being spirit-beings are also called *pneumata*.

Thus, we have simply "*the pneumata*" (Matt. viii. 16); "unclean *pneumata*" (Matt. x. 1); "*the pneuma* the unclean*"*(Luke ix. 42); "the unclean demon" (Luke

---

* This is the very same construction (only in the very opposite sense) that is used of "the Holy Spirit." He is called "*the pneuma the holy* :" while this demon (Luke ix. 42) is called "*the pneuma the unclean*."

iv. 33); "a dumb *pneuma* (Mark ix. 17); a pneuma of infirmity" : *i.e.*, causing infirmity (Luke xiii. 11); "a *pneuma* of Python" (Acts xvi. 16).

XIII.   *Pneuma* is used also of the RESURRECTION BODY, as being something distinct from a purely *human* body on the one hand ; and distinct also from a spiritual or *angelic* creation on the other hand.   Angels never had a human body ; but the raised and changed Saints will have had human bodies; and hence, in resurrection, they will be made glorious like their risen Lord's (Phil. iii. 21).   Human bodies are "flesh and blood" (for "the blood is the life" of a human body).   Christ's resurrection body was not thus purely human.   It was a glorious body.   It was "flesh and bones," which He distinctly says a *pneuma*, or purely spirit-being, has not.   "A *pneuma* hath not flesh and bones as ye see me have" (Luke xxiv. 39).

The resurrection body of the saints will be a *pneuma*-body (or a spirit-body); and yet not identical with that of angels or of demons, or with the present human body. On this, see 1 Cor. xv. 45, which will be discussed and enlarged on, in the list of passages, to follow.

Here are thirteen different usages of the word *pneuma*. Each one is quite distinct from the other.   But in all these thirteen cases the word *pneuma* is used alone.

There is still the presence and absence of the definite article ("the") to be observed.   And the meaning of its use or omission must be determined by the context.   The article is not used at hap-hazard, or by chance; but by the Divine author of the Scripture in all His Divine perfection.   It may denote the Holy Spirit; or it may be used only grammatically in order to refer to what has been said before in the immediate context.   Examples of this we shall see as we come to the various passages involved in this enquiry.

The next, the usage with "*hagion*" (*holy*), is the most important of all, and is fraught with far reaching consequences as affecting traditional doctrines and beliefs.

XIV.   The fourteenth example of the usage of πνεῦμα (*pneuma*) *spirit* in the New Testament is its combination with the word ἅγιον (*hagion*) *holy*.

Of this combination there are three kinds:

1. When neither of the two words has the article: *e.g.*, *pneuma hagion*.

2. When both of them have the article: *e.g.*, *the pneuma the holy* [*pneuma*].

3. When only one of them has the article: *e.g.*, *the holy pneuma*.

Each of these must be distinct from the others; for surely the perfection of the Divine *Word* involves the perfection of the Divine *words*.   The Scripture is made up of " words . . . which the Holy Ghost teacheth."

Surely God not only means what he says, but He must have a distinct meaning for everything He says.

If we translate them all "The Holy Spirit," inserting the article (" the ") in the English, where there is none in the Greek, are we not confusing what the Divine Author has distinguished?   Are we not treating His words with disrespect, and this to our own hindrance and loss?

If, when there is no article in the Greek, we take the liberty of interpolating one in the English, and at the same time take the further liberty of putting a capital " H " and a capital "S," are we not interpreting instead of translating?

And if we translate *pneuma hagion* "the Holy Spirit," there is no stronger expression left which we can use when both the words, in the Greek, have the definite article.

This shows us that these two different expressions cannot, and must not, be rendered in exactly the same way in the English.

Yet, out of the fifty places where *pneuma hagion* occurs, this is the rendering generally given to it in both the A.V. and R.V. The great liberty is taken, by both Versions, of designedly adding the article "the" in the English when God has designedly omitted it in the Greek; and of using capital letters without any authority whatever.

Surely language becomes useless for the purpose of revelation if we thus confuse two things between which God has set so great a difference.

In vain has He used the Greek *presbyteros* (*elder*) and *hierus* (*a sacrificing priest*) if we render them both by the one word "priest."

In vain did the framers of the "Thirty-nine Articles of Religion" use *presbyterus* (*elder*) and *sacerdos* (*a sacrificing priest*) if both words are to be translated by the one word "Priest."*

In vain has God used "*pneuma hagion*" (without any definite articles), and "*the pneuma the holy*" (with two

---

*As *Sacerdos* is rendered in Art. xxxi., and *Presbyteros* is rendered in Art. xxxvi. The reader must remember that the Thirty-nine Articles were originally written in Latin; and that we have only an English Translation in the Prayer Book. Some Sacramentarians, not noting this, appeal to Art. xxxi. as recognising the sacrificing priest. So it does; but it is speaking of Romish priests, and, therefore, the word used is "*sacerdos*." But when Art. xxxvi. uses the word "Priest" in the sense of "Elders" or of the Christian Ministry, it always uses the word PRESBYTER in the Latin. This fact is hidden by translating both the words "priest."

articles) if we render them both, in the same way, " the Holy Spirit."

Surely we shall not be charged with heresy for believing that God's Word is perfect. Rather may others be charged with carelessness when so little care is taken to distinguish what God has caused to differ.

PNEUMA HAGION

When we have examined all the fifty passages where this expression (*pneuma hagion*) occurs, we shall find this to be the general result, that it is never used in the sense in which (*to pneuma to hagion*) " the pneuma the holy " is used: that is to say, it is never used of the Holy Spirit, but always of what He does; it is never used of the Giver, but always of His gifts and operations.

A careful study of all the fifty occurrences of *pneuma hagion* establishes the fact that this is the uniform usage of the expression.

" That which is born of THE *pneuma* [the Giver] is *pneuma* [His gift]" (John iii. 6).

First, we have the Divine *source*, and then that which comes from that Divine *source*. (See this passage in the list of passages to follow.)

If we ask, How, then, are we to render "*pneuma hagion*"? we might answer, " holy spirit," without the definite article " the "; and with a small " h," and a small " s." But when this is said, and done, we are not much forwarder in gaining a clear understanding as to what is meant by the words; or in expressing the exact sense intended to be conveyed to our minds.

Happily, we are not left to our own ingenuity in discovering a suitable rendering; nor are we dependent on any man for him to tell us what this expression means.

We have the Lord's own definition. He gives us the

equivalent, which settles the matter for us; and leaves us in no doubt as to what is meant by *pneuma hagion*.

This exact meaning is obtained by comparing Acts i. 4, 5, with Luke xxiv. 49.

In Acts i. 4, the Lord commanded the Apostles "that they should not depart from Jerusalem, but wait for the promise* of the Father, which (saith he) ye have heard of me."

They had heard it, as recorded in Luke xxiv. 49, when He said, " Behold, I send the promise of my Father upon you: but tarry ye in the city of Jerusalem, until ye be endued with POWER FROM ON HIGH."†

This was what the Father had promised. And the Lord goes on, in the next verse (Acts i. 5), to further explain this by saying that "John truly baptized with water; but ye shall be baptized with *pneuma hagion* not many days hence."

In these two passages we have the key to the meaning we are to put upon the expression *pneuma hagion ;* because, in both passages (Luke xxiv. 49 and Acts i. 4, 5) the Lord is speaking of *the same thing*, *viz.*, "the promise of the Father."

In Luke xxiv. 49 He calls this "promise," "power from on high."

In Acts i. 5 He calls this same "promise," " *pneuma hagion*."

Therefore, we have this foundation and self-evident truth that *pneuma hagion* is identical with " *power from on high*."

It is impossible for us to get away from this fact. It makes us independent of all human teachers, and sets us free from all man's opinions.

---

* "Promise" is here put (by *Metonymy* of the adjunct) for the *fulfilment* of the promise.

† δύναμις ἐξ ὕψους (*dunamis ex hypsous*) *power out of*, or *from*, *on high: i.e., from heaven*, or *from above*.

We have it, here, on Divine Authority, that "power from on high "* is to be taken as the equivalent of the Greek, *pneuma hagion*, whenever we meet with it.

This " power "† may be manifested in different forms. It may be " power " for service, for speech, for miracles, for wisdom and knowledge, for teaching, or for whatever it may be needed.

It may sometimes be well rendered "Divine power," or " spiritual power," or " spiritual gifts."

But, however we may mention *pneuma hagion*, there is one thing certain: it never means the Holy Spirit

---

* It is interesting to note that, in this very Gospel, Luke claims to have this " power." In Luke i. 3 he says that he had perfect understanding of these things "from above." Not "from the very first " (A.V.), or "from the first " (R.V.). The Greek here is ἄνωθεν (*anōthen*) *from above*, and should be so rendered, as it is in

> Jas. i. 17 : " Every good gift and every perfect gift cometh down *from above* " (not " from the first.")

> Jas. iii. 15 : " This wisdom descendeth not *from above*."
>   17 : " The wisdom that is *from above*."

> John iii. 3, 7 : " Ye must be born *from above* " (see margin). The A.V. renders it " again " ; the R.V. "anew." Both Versions have "*from above* " in the margin.

> Luke xxiv. 49 expresses the same truth, though another word is used to describe it.

> So, in ch. i. 3, Luke had his " understanding " *from above*, and that is why it was " perfect."

The word rendered *power* in these cases is always δύναμις (*dunamis*) *inherent power*, not so much power put forth, but *power possessed, capability*. It thus differs from ἐξουσία (*exousia*) *authority* (Matt. vii. 29. John i. 12 ; v. 27, etc.) ; and from κράτος (*kratos*) *strength* put forth (Luke i. 51. Eph. i. 19. Col. i. 11, etc.). Here it is *dunamis* (from which we have *dynamite, dynamic* force, etc. (See Matt. vi. 13. Rev. v. 12. Luke xxix. 49. Acts i. 8), for it is this *power* which is imparted, and with which those who receive *pneuma hagion* are said to be " endued." The Greek "endued" means *clothed with* power, in Luke xxiv. 49. (See Acts xii. 21, where it is rendered *arrayed*. 1 Cor. xv. 53, 54, *put on*. 2 Cor. v. 3, etc.).

Himself, but always His Divine " power" as put forth
and manifested in various ways and operations, and in
His bestowal of spiritual " gifts " or powers as described
in 1 Cor. xii. 7-11.

When this "promise of the Father " was originally
fulfilled in Acts ii. 4, the two are carefully distinguished.
In the very same verse the two are mentioned together,
and we are distinctly told that the Apostles " were all
filled with *pneuma hagion* [the gift], and began to speak
with other tongues [one of His gifts] as THE *Pneuma*
[the Giver] gave them utterance."

This proves that the two are perfectly distinct and are
not to be confused. First we have the GIFT called
pneuma hagion (without the article); then we have, in
the very same verse, the GIVER mentioned (with the
definite article), "THE *Pneuma*," to denote the great
Giver of this wonderful " power from on high."   " Speaking with tongues " is stated (in 1 Cor. xii. 10, 30) to be
one of the gifts of the Holy Spirit; and this was the
special gift bestowed at Pentecost.

Another thing comes out in this passage (Acts ii. 4).
The Greek is " they were all filled *of-pneuma hagion* " : in
other words, the Greek verb *to fill* is always followed by
the Genitive case of that with which anything or anyone
is *filled*.*   That is to say, the Greeks always said they
were " filled of" anything, whereas we, in our English
idiom, say " filled with."

---

* See Luke iv. 28, " filled with (Gen.) wrath " (Gr., of-wrath).
Luke v. 26, " filled with (Gen.) fear " (Gr., of-fear).   Luke vi. 11,
"filled with (Gen.) madness" (Gr., of-madness).   Acts iii. 10, "filled
with (Gen.) wonder " (Gr., of-wonder).   Acts v. 17, " filled with
(Gen.) indignation " (Gr., of-indignation).   Acts xiii. 43, " filled
with (Gen.) envy " (Gr., of-envy).   Acts xiii. 52, " filled with (Gen.)
joy " (Gr., of-joy).   Acts xix. 29, " filled with (Gen.) confusion "
(Gr., of-confusion).

See, for example, Luke i. 15, " He shall be filled with (Gen.) *pneuma hagion* " (Greek, of-*pneuma hagion*). It is the same in verses 41, 67; iv. 1. Acts iv. 8, 31 ; * vii. 55 ; ix. 17 ; xi. 24 ; xiii. 9.

In all these passages there is no article in the Greek, and there should be none in the English, nor should there be any capital letters. Each time, the Genitive case is used after the word *to fill*, to denote that wherewith they were filled : viz., " power from on high " : *i.e.*, spiritual or divine power.

We ought also to note, in connection with the working of this grammatical law, that the Accusative case is used of the place, person, or thing that is filled. See Acts v. 28, " Ye have filled Jerusalem (Acc.) with (Gen., lit. *of*) your teaching."

But when the person, agent, or instrument that fills is to be mentioned, then the Dative case is used ; or, the Preposition (ἐν, *en*), followed by the Dative case (ἐν πνεύματι, *en pneumati*) *by* or *through* [*the*] *Spirit* (the article being latent after the Preposition, and not required to be used unless for special emphasis). See Eph. ii. 22, " Ye are builded together for an habitation of God through [or by] the Spirit " (ἐν πνεύματι, *en pneumati*). This is the expression in Eph. v. 18, be filled, " through (or by) the Spirit," where it is again ἐν πνεύματι (*en pneumati*), and not the genitive case, as in all other passages. It was not the Person " with " whom they were to be filled, but by or through whom they were to be filled. They were not to be filled through (or by) wine, in which there is excess (of talkativeness), but by the Spirit who, when He fills with His " power from on high," enables us to " speak " with spiritual conversation.

* The Critical Greek Texts add one article here and change the order of the words, but the article is grammatical and refers to the original gift of ch. ii. 4.

If it meant what it is popularly supposed to teach, the word "spirit" would, of necessity, be in the Genitive case, "be filled of-the Spirit," but this is not what it says. We are to be filled "by the Spirit." He is the *filler*, and He fills with His gifts and His power: just as in Eph. ii. 22, where He is the *builder*, He builds the Holy Temple of the Lord with "living stones," sprinkled with the blood.

See further under Eph. v. 18, in its place, in the list to be given below.

It is the same when the adjective "full" is used.* "Look ye out among you seven men of honest report, full of-*pneuma hagion* (Gen.), and of wisdom (Gen.), whom we may appoint over this business" (Acts vi. 3).

The A.V. and R.V. say, "full of the Holy Ghost." If this be correct, then it is clear that He does not include wisdom in Himself: and that, according to this, a man may be full of the Holy Ghost Himself, and yet be destitute of wisdom.

No, they wanted men "full of Divine power," or *spiritual gifts*, but, of all the spiritual gifts, they wanted specially "the gift of wisdom," for it was a "business" matter over which they were to be set.

A man may be a very spiritual man, with gifts of speaking and of working miracles ; but he may be, at the same time, very foolish in business matters.

They chose (verse 5) the seven, and among them they chose Stephen, who not only had the gift of "wisdom" as part of this "power from on high," but he was "a man full of-faith" (Gen.) and of-*pneuma hagion* (Gen.).

Then we read in verse 8, "and Stephen, full of-faith (Gen.) and of-power (Gen.) did great wonders and miracles among the people." "Faith and power," as well as "wisdom," are thus included in this "power

---

* In this case the English idiom is the same as the Greek, for we say "full of" as they did.

from on high "; so that Stephen had other spiritual gifts beside " wisdom." He had the gift of " faith" (1 Cor. xii. 9), and the gift of " the working of miracles " (1 Cor. xii. 10). The result of Stephen's ministry was that his enemies " were not able to resist the wisdom and *the pneuma* by which he spake"* (verse 10). Here, although the article is used with *pneuma*, it is used only grammatically, in order to refer back to the *pneuma hagion* of verses 3 and 5. It is not the Holy Spirit who is meant, hence the A.V. rightly uses a small " s."† We learn from this that Stephen's address in chapter vii. was inspired.

Luke xi. 13 is another passage which is generally regarded as referring to " the Holy Spirit," and is so translated with the article and capital letters, both in the A.V. and R.V. " If ye then, being evil, know how to give good gifts unto your children : how much more shall your heavenly Father give *pneuma hagion* to them that ask Him." It is, here, simply *pneuma hagion*, and means *spiritual gifts*, or " good things " (as in the parallel passage, Matt. vii. 11). See further on this passage, in its place, in the list to be given below.

Again, we have another proof of this " power from on high " being *pneuma hagion*, in Acts viii. 19, 20. Simon Magus said to Peter, " Give me also this power, that on whomsoever I lay hands, he may receive *pneuma hagion*. But Peter said unto him, thy money perish with thee, because thou hast thought that THE GIFT OF GOD may be purchased with money." So that here, again, *pneuma hagion* is actually called "God's gift," and must not be confused with the Giver of the gift. It is the Divine "power," and not the Divine Giver of the power, the Holy Spirit.

---

* Though his enemies, who knew and understood all he said, " could not resist " him, critics to-day do so, though they have not that knowledge.

† The R.V. has a capital "S."

As the " gift of God," *pneuma hagion* is spoken of as being " received."

In John xx. 22, the Lord Jesus breathed on the Apostles, and said " Receive ye *pneuma hagion*." Not " the Holy Ghost." There is no article : and it is not the Spirit Himself who is meant ; He had not yet come ; for the Lord Jesus had not gone to the Father. " When He is (or shall have) come " (John xvi. 13), marks a definite moment of coming, as fulfilled in Acts ii. 4. It means, here, " Receive ye power from on high" : *i.e.,* Divine power, Spiritual power, Spiritual gifts, such as Stephen afterwards received: See Acts vi. 3, 5, 8, 10 (compare Isa. xi. 2, 3).

Sometimes, a fuller expression is used (with the article) : *i.e., the holy pneuma ; viz.,* the holy "power from on high," as the fulfilment of " the promise of the Father " : but even in this case the article may be only grammatical, pointing back to Acts ii. 4. In Acts x. 45, the fuller expression of verse 44 is spoken of as " the gift " given by " the Holy Spirit." So that we have the " *gift* " in verse 44, and the *giver* in verse 45. This " *gift* " is explained and described in verse 46 as being the special gift of tongues, and refers back, as we have said to ch. ii. 4.

In Acts viii. 19, 20, it is specially called " the gift of God," as we have seen above.

Some Bishops to-day, at " Confirmation," profess to give " the Holy Spirit." As they misunderstand the expression *pneuma hagion*, they do not profess to give spiritual power or gifts ; we could soon test them if they did, and be convinced that no such power or gifts were bestowed ; and that it really was only an " imposition " of hands ! But as it is the Holy Spirit Himself whom they profess to give, it is impossible for us to judge one way or the other. (See further on John xx. 22, in the list to follow).

We have the same special expression in Acts xi. In verse 15 we have "*the pneuma the hagion,*" *i.e.,* the "gift" (the articles referring back to ch. ii. 4); and then, in verse 17, we have the Divine Giver mentioned. Thus the context shows how the articles are to be interpreted.

The Lord Jesus Himself so speaks of it in John iv. 10 "If thou knewest the gift of God," *i.e.,* the gift of spiritual life and Divine power with all its blessed manifestations, capabilities, and possibilities.

In Eph. iii. 7, it is called "the gift of the grace of God": *i.e.,* God's gracious gift, or His gift of grace. And, as we have seen from Acts viii. 19, 20, the one phrase is thus used for the other.

As this *pneuma hagion* comes from "on high," so it is spoken of as "falling on" those who received it (see Acts viii. 15, 16; x. 44). It was not the Holy Spirit Himself who "fell on" people; but He caused His power and His gifts that were bestowed by Him to fall on them "from on high."

It is the same with the verb *to pour out*. How can a Person be poured out? It is impossible. But a Person can be said to pour out His "gifts"; and that is what is meant by the expression.

For the same reason *pneuma hagion* is said to be "received"; because it is the *gift*, and not the Giver who is received, as in John xx. 22.

The *usage* of pneuma in the Acts of the Apostles is special,* and is quite distinct from the peculiarly Pauline usage in the Church Epistles. This will be seen on a careful examination of all the passages in the list to follow.

In the Acts nearly all the expressions, more or less full, denote that "power from on high" with which the

---

* *Nineteen* out of the fifty occurrences of "*pneuma hagion*" are in this one book, the Acts.

book opens, *viz.*, the Divine energy put forth; of the manifestations of which the book is so full that it has sometimes been spoken of as "the Acts of the Holy Spirit."

Even where the definite article is used, it does not necessarily or always denote the Giver; for the article may be used, as we have said, only grammatically for the purpose of identifying the word with a previous mention of *pneuma hagion*. This is the case in Acts viii. 18,* compared with verses 15, 16. In the same way Acts xi. 15 may refer back to ch. ii. 4; as the spirit will, just after, be spoken of in verse 17 as "the like gift": *viz.*, the gift mentioned in chap. ii. 4.

On the other hand, the article is never used with the expression when it is associated with "baptism." Here, it is always *pneuma hagion*, *i.e.*, the spiritual in contrast with the material medium; and not the Holy Ghost. Christ is the baptizer, and not the Holy Spirit: and He baptises with *pneuma hagion*.

It is *pneuma hagion* that is contrasted with *water* as the element with which the believer is baptized. It is the *spiritual* element in contrast with the *material* element. (See Luke iii. 16. Acts i. 5; xi. 16.)

Passing on to Acts xix. 2, we read that Paul asks certain disciples at Ephesus whether they had received *pneuma hagion* at the time when† they believed. And they answered "we have not so much as heard whether there be [such a thing as] *pneuma hagion*."

They must surely have heard of the Holy Spirit; but, Ephesus was a long way from Jerusalem and Cæsarea where these spiritual gifts had been first given; and these

---

* See this passage in its place in the list, for the various readings involved in it.

† There is no word for "since" in the Greek. It is simply the participle, and means *on believing*: *i.e.*, *when ye believed.*

believers had not heard about them. See further on this passage in its place in the list below.

From all that has been said of *pneuma hagion* it will be seen that the usage of the expression marks it off very distinctly from the Holy Spirit; and thus distinguishes the gift from the Giver.

As, however, in most of the passages the Translators and Revisers have taken the liberty of inserting the definite article, " the "; and used capital letters; it has been, and is, generally believed to refer to the Holy Spirit.

The importance of our work will be at once seen: as it will enable the ordinary English reader to distinguish not only what *pneuma* means in all its 385 occurrences, but what *pneuma hagion* means in the fifty places where we meet with this expression.

It may, however, be asked, How are we to understand what is meant as it concerns our own individual experience? How does all this affect what is spoken of, theologically, as the " indwelling of the Holy Spirit "?

The answer is that the difficulty is partly of our own creating; from our not carefully noting the exact language of Scripture; partly from our clinging to "tradition"; and partly from the failure of human terminology when used of Divine truths.

Words are but counters on which we agree to put a certain value respectively. These words are human and *finite*; but the things connected with our subject are *infinite*. It is impossible, truly and exactly, to express Divine realities with human words, or infinite truths with finite words.

We speak of " the Person " of the Holy Spirit, but what do we mean? What is the idea conveyed to our mind by this collocation of words? What is the actual sense of " person " used in this connection?

" Person" denotes an individual. The word is from the Latin "*per*," *through*, and "*sonare*," *to sound*, and was used of *the mask through* which the actor's voice *sounded*, as he represented a particular personage. Hence the *usage* of the word always refers to *individuality*.

The Christian Creeds do not speak of "three Persons " as though they were three Gods. We are not Polytheists but Trinitarians; *i.e.*, we believe in "a Trinity in Unity, and Unity in Trinity."

" Three in One ; and One in Three "

It is not therefore correct to speak of the Holy Spirit as a Person apart from His being God Himself.

Christ can be spoken of as a " Person," for He is " God manifest in the flesh," and therefore individualized. Hence, He can be spoken of as localized now, as sitting on the Father's throne (Rev. iii. 21), and hereafter, at His advent, as sitting " on the throne of His glory " (Matt. xxv. 31).

But, in the Scripture, the Holy Spirit is neither called nor spoken of as "a Person." He is spoken of as " God," (Compare Acts v. 3 with verse 4).

God is *pneuma*, and there is no common ground between flesh and *pneuma*. Hence we know Him objectively, in Christ, as our Creator and Redeemer ; and we know Him subjectively, within us, by realizing His presence there in His gracious operations and gifts.

The Pauline teaching, as it is called, is distinctly in advance of the truth that is revealed in the Old Testament ; or rather, we should say, the Divine revelation by Paul speaks not only of a power proceeding from God, and working in the hearts of His people, but that of God Himself " working in " them (Phil. ii. 13), and clothing them with His "power." This is why it is called "power from on high" (Luke xxiv. 49).

Dr. Candlish puts it thus:* "The Spirit of God is not in his (Paul's) view an independent personality; that is not implied in the doctrine of the personality of the Spirit; but, as the spirit of a man is to man, so, according to Paul, the Spirit of God is to God; in one sense the same, but in another sense distinct. The principle of the Christian life is not a mere impersonal power, but God Himself in a mysterious way dwelling and working in the soul. But it is God working in man to lead him to God as He is above him; hence the Spirit of God that works in him must be distinguished from God, yet not as a different being; but just as the spirit or mind of a man may be distinguished from the man, and may be said to know the things of a man (1 Cor. ii. 10-16)."

In the Divine spiritual "gifts," "ministrations," and "operations," we have a marvellous and mysterious testimony to the Biblical doctrine of the Trinity. We recognise them as the work of one Spirit, one Lord (Christ), and one God and Father of all (1 Cor. xii. 4-6, compare Eph. iv. 4-13).

The Holy Spirit is God; and God is omnipresent. Yet, in the Tabernacle and Temple of old, His presence was manifested by the miraculous shining of the Shechinah; so real, that God Himself was said to "dwell" there.

Even so in all His people to-day His presence is manifested by His miraculous operations and gifts, so real, that God is said to dwell in us; so real, that the new nature which is begotten of "The *Pneuma*" is itself

* *The Work of the Holy Spirit.* By James S. Candlish, D.D. T. & T. Clark), p. 26.

pneuma and Divine. Hence, in 2 Pet. i. 4, those who possess this, are stated to be " partakers of the Divine nature."

There is no need for us to increase the difficulties necessarily inherent in so great a subject, by introducing a word which the Scripture does not once use of the Holy Spirit. He is never called a " Person " in Scripture ; and we only create a difficulty when we use the language of Theology instead of the words of God.

Surely the fact is great enough for us without weakening the force of this wondrous truth, or losing sight of the glorious reality.

God is in us ; and the evidence of this to us is that, as the *Pneuma*, He there begets *pneuma*, and performs His new creation work, with all its consequent bestowal of graces and gifts.

In the various passages in which the word *pneuma* is used, sometimes the reference is to Himself as the *worker*, and sometimes it is to the *work* which He performs. And it is our business to " search the Scriptures," and find out all that He has revealed in connection with this great subject.

It is peculiarly a matter of Divine revelation : for, apart from the Word of God we can know nothing whatever about it. We are wise, or we must " err," according as we know or do not " know the Scriptures."

We are now ready to consider each passage by itself : and we propose to give each, and to make the list complete and exhaustive. Each expression (or *use*) will be given, and the particular *usage* of the word, or words, or phrase will be carefully noted. Then, when we examine each in the light of the context, we shall learn what, in the God-breathed Word, has been " written for our learning."

We must be prepared to *unlearn*, as well as to *learn ;* for much of what we have received on this subject, as well as on others, is from tradition, and rests only on human authority. This, as we well know, is more likely to mislead us than to guide us aright.

We cannot do more, or do better, than put our readers in possession of all the facts, and give them the whole of the *data.* The responsibility will then rest entirely with themselves as to the use they make of the information. With this complete list in their hands they will be independent of man, and be able to say with David:

> " I have more understanding than my teachers :
> For thy testimonies are my meditation."
> " How sweet are thy words unto my taste !
> Yea, sweeter than honey to my mouth ! "
> " Therefore I love thy commandments above gold:
> Yea, above fine gold " (Ps. cxix. 99, 103, 127).

We repeat that we are dealing with the " words " of God, and not merely with the " Word." We are taking pleasure in examining the perfections of the Divine workmanship (Ps. cxi. 2). We are bringing, as it were, the spiritual microscope into use. But, with all this, we can never with our finite minds exhaust the wonders of either the words or works of our God. We shall be able to say with David (Ps. cxix. 162):

> " I rejoice at thy word,
>
> As one that findeth great spoil."

God has been graciously pleased to give us a revelation in *writing.* That writing consists of *words.* And these words are " God-breathed " (2 Tim. iii. 16).

In the exact and perfect precision in the use and usage of the word *pneuma* and its various combinations, we have the greatest proof of " verbal inspiration." If we slur over these differences and these varied expressions, and treat them as though they were used by chance, or at haphazard, instead of being perfect and Divine, it is clear that we must err, not distinguishing what God has made to differ. One of our duties with regard to the Word of God is to try, or

> "*Prove the things that differ*"*

If we would abound in knowledge and in all discernment, and be sincere and without offence till the day of Christ (Phil. i. 9, 10), then we must obey this precept; and try, and prove, and test, the things, even the words and expressions which God, in His Word, has Himself "made to differ.

References in Which *Pneuma* Occurs in the New Testament

We now give a complete list of all the passages where the word πνεῦμα (*pneuma*) *spirit*, occurs in the New Testament.

If our readers will mark in their Bibles the use and usage in each case, they will have all the information that can be given, and that is needed to enable them to judge for themselves as to the interpretation of the word, and of the passage.

MATTHEW

Matt. 1:18 " She was found with child by *pneuma hagion*." Here the article may be latent, implied after the preposition ἐκ (*ek*) *of* or *by* the " power from on high " put forth by the Holy Spirit. Compare Luke i. 35. The A.V. of 1611 has " H " and " G." The R.V. and current editions of A.V. have capital letters.

Matt. 1:20 " That which is in her is begotten by *pneuma hagion*." Here it is power put forth by the Holy Spirit, agreeing with verse 18, and with Luke i. 35 (see ch. i. 18, above). The capital letters are the same as in verse 18.

Matt. 3:11 John said : " I indeed baptize you with water unto repentance : but he that cometh after me is mightier than I, . . . he shall baptize you with *pneuma hagion* and fire."

This is the Figure *Hendiadys*; by which, two words are used, but one thing is meant ; the latter noun becoming a superlative adjective. The English idiom would be : ' He shall baptize you with *pneuma hagion*, yea, with a burning [*pueuma hagion*], that will refine, and purge, and purify the People of Israel.' It is *judgment* that is being spoken of by John, not mercy or grace (see verses 7-10, and compare Is. iv. 4 and Mal. iii. 2).

This refining and purging by judgment will precede the cleansing and purifying by grace, which will take place after it. That is characterised by "*pneuma* and water" (see John iii. 5 below, and compare Ezek. xxxvi. 25-27, etc.).

In 1 Cor. ii. 4 we have "*pneuma* and power"; *i.e.*, powerful spiritual demonstration (the Figure *Hendiadys* again).

The capital letters are used as in chap. i. 18.

Matt. 3:16   " He saw *the× pneuma* of God descending like a dove." Here, the articles, and the context together, show that it is the Holy Spirit Himself who is symbolised by the bodily form of a dove.   The A.V. and R.V. both have " S."

Matt. 4:1   " Then was Jesus led up of *the pneuma* "; *i.e.*, the Holy Spirit, as in chap. iii. 15. This is shown by the article being used as well as the preposition ὑπό (*hypo*) by.   The A.V. of 1611 had a large " S," as the R.V. has.   But, strange to say, the current editions of the A.V. have a small " s."

Matt. 5:3   " Blessed are the poor in *the pneuma* [of them] " : *i.e.*, in their spirit.   Or, poor as to their spirit. Here the article is used grammatically, to indicate the

---

* Tischendorf, and Westcott and Hort, omit the articles here before Spirit and God. Alford puts them in brackets.

possessive pronoun, and *pneuma* is used as denoting *character*. Character is spoken of as *pneuma* because it is invisible; in contrast to that which is visible. This verse, when compared with verse 8, may refer to *mental endowments* of which we are apt to be so proud; and the other to those *affections of the feelings* by which we are so apt to be led astray.

Here the A.V. and R.V. have a small " s."

Matt. 8:16 " He cast out *the pneumata** with His word." Here, evil spirits are meant.

A.V. and R.V. have " s," as in all cases where evil spirits are clearly meant.

Matt. 10:1 " He gave them power (Greek, *authority*) over unclean *pneumata*." Same as chap. viii. 16.

Matt. 10:20 " For it is not ye that speak, but *the pneuma* of your Father which speaketh in you." This looks as if it were the original " promise of the Father " referred to by Christ in Luke xxiv. 49. But, on comparing it with Mark xiii. 11, it it clear that it is the Holy Spirit, for there it is *the pneuma the holy*.

The A.V. and R.V. both have " S."

Matt. 12:18 " I will put my *pneuma* upon him." (Lit., *the pneuma* of me).

This is the fulfilment of Isa. xlii. 1-4, where the A.V. and R.V. both have a small " s." There is also a reference to Isa. xi. 2, where it refers to the spiritual gifts of " wisdom," and " understanding," and " counsel," and " might," and " knowledge," and " godly fear," and " quick understanding." These are not seven Holy Spirits, but seven of His gifts (See under Rev. i. 4).

---

* Here we have put *pneumata*, as it is the plural form of the Greek *pneuma*. So in all subsequent similar cases.

The A.V., consistently with Isa. xlii. 1, puts a small "s" here. But the R.V. has a capital "S" here, notwithstanding the small "s" in Isa. xlii. 1.

Matt. 12:28   "If I by *pneuma* of God (or, by God's *pneuma*) cast out demons." Here, the Genitive denotes apposition ("If I by *pneuma, i.e.,* God). There is no article: but it is not required grammatically, being latent after the preposition. "*Pneuma Theou,*" here, is to be distinguished from Rom. viii. 14, where there is no preposition as there is here. Both A.V. and R.V. put the article and use capital letters.

Verses 31 and 32 clearly show that the Holy Spirit is meant, and thus prove that He is "God."

Matt. 12:31   "But of (or concerning, Gen. of relation) *the pneuma*, blasphemy will not be forgiven."

Matt. 12:32   "Whosoever speaketh against the *pneuma the holy*, it will not be forgiven him."

Here, in both these verses, the Holy Spirit is meant. What this blasphemy was is clearly explained in verse 24. It is ascribing to Beelzebub (*i.e.,* Satan himself) that which was wrought by the Holy Spirit.

The A.V. of 1611 had "H" and "G" in both verses. The R.V. has "H" and "S."

Matt. 12:43   "When the unclean *pneuma* is gone out of a man." Here, *pneuma* is used of an evil spirit.

Matt. 12:45   "He taketh with him seven other *pneumata* more wicked than himself."

Here again, evil spirits are meant; and we learn that there are degrees of wickedness among them. See under Luke xi. 24-26.

Matt. 14:26   The word rendered "spirit" in this verse, is not *pneuma* at all. It is φάντασμα (*phantasma*), *a phantasm* or *phantom.* It occurs only here and Mark vi. 49.

Matt. 22:43 " How then doth David by [the] *pneuma* call him Lord ?"

Here the preposition (ἐν, *en*) *by*, does not necessitate presence of the article, grammatically ; so that it denotes the Holy Spirit speaking through David. Hence we have in this passage (Ps. cx. 1) David's voice, and David's pen, but *not David's words*. This is the Scriptural account of inspiration, and renders all other definitions unnecessary. Compare Mark xii. 36.

The A.V. has "s"; but the R.V. puts " S," and adds the definite article.

Matt. 26:41 " *The pneuma* indeed is willing, but the flesh is weak." Here the article is used, both with "*pneuma*" and "flesh," to mark them as the subject, and to set them in contrast. The *pneuma*, therefore, here, will denote what is invisible : *i.e.*, the mind and will of man, in contrast to his flesh. It cannot mean the Holy Spirit, although it has the article ; nor can it mean His spiritual gifts. The A.V. and R.V. both have "s."

Matt. 27:50 " Jesus, when he had cried again with a loud voice, yielded up *the pneuma* [of him]: *i.e.*, His *pneuma*."

Here it is used psychologically of man's nature, according to Ps. xxxi. 5, and Ecc. xii. 7. (Compare Gen. ii. 7.)

The A.V. has a small "g" (ghost), and the R.V. a small " s " (spirit).

Matt. 28:19 " Baptizing them in the name of the Father, and of the Son, and of *the holy pneuma* "; *i e.*, the Holy Spirit.* This is to be carefully distinguished

---

* These words are contained in every Greek MS. known, and

from being baptized with *pneuma hagion* (See below, Mark i. 8).

The A.V. of 1611, had a small " h "; but current editions, with R.V., have " H."

MARK

Mark 1:8 " He shall baptize you with *pneuma hagion* "; *i.e.*, with " power from on high," or with Divine and Spiritual gifts which are far better than

---

are, therefore, on documentary evidence, beyond suspicion : but yet there is one great difficulty with regard to them.

The difficulty is that, the Apostles themselves never obeyed this command ; and in the rest of the New Testament there is no hint as to its ever having been obeyed by anyone. Baptism was always in the name of the one person of the Lord Jesus.

> Acts ii. 38. " Be baptized in the name of Jesus Christ."
> Acts viii. 16. "They were baptized in the name of the Lord Jesus."
> Acts x. 48. " He commanded them to be baptized in the name of the Lord."
> Acts xix. 5. "They were baptized in the name of the Lord Jesus."

It is difficult to suppose that there would have been this universal disregard of so clear a command, if it had ever been given ; or it ever really formed part of the primitive text.

It is a question, therefore, whether we have here, something beyond the reach of the science, or the powers of ordinary Textual Criticism.

As to the Greek MSS. there are none beyond the fourth Century, and it seems clear that the Syrian part of the Church knew nothing of these words.

Eusebius quotes this verse no less than *eighteen times*, and always quotes it in this form, " Go ye into all the world and make disciples of all nations." He omits all reference to "baptizing them in the name of the Father, Son and Holy Ghost."

Now Eusebius, the great Ecclesiastical historian, died in 340 A.D., and his work belonged, therefore, in part to the *third*

material water. The contrast here lies between what is spiritual and what is material.

The A.V. of 1611, had a small "h"; but current editions, with R.V., have "H." Both add the definite article.

Mark 1:10 "He saw *the pneuma*, like a dove, descending upon him."

This is the same as Matt. iii. 16. Both A.V. and R.V. have "S."

---

century. Moreover, he lived in one of the greatest Christian Libraries of that day. If the Greek MS. there contained these words it seems impossible that he could have quoted this verse eighteen times without including them.

Professor Lake (now of the University of Leiden) and Mr. Conybeare have called attention to this fact, and shown that neither Justin Martyr (who died in 165 A.D.), nor Aphraates, of Nisibis (who flourished in Syria, 340 A.D.), knew anything of these words.

It looks, therefore, as though the words got into the text (perhaps from the margin) in the Church of North Africa; and that the Syrian Churches did not have them in the MSS. at their disposal.

The point is interesting. The difficulty is there. And if there be any truth in Professor Lake's argument, then that would be a reasonable explanation of it.

If this be not the explanation, then we submit that the verse must be rightly divided, and the command must be understood as referring entirely to the future preaching of "the Gospel of the kingdom" in the coming new Dispensation; and as having no place in this present Church period, which is the Dispensation of Grace.

It is clear that some sort of "dividing" of the word of truth is necessary, for the whole verse as it stands is in conflict with Matt. x. 5 "go not into the way of the Gentiles." If those words refer to the then Dispensation, when the Kingdom was at hand; then Matt. xxviii. 19 may refer to the coming Dispensation, when the Kingdom shall be again proclaimed, and then the "all power," given unto Christ, shall be exercised in heaven and on earth.

Mark 1:12 "And immediately *the pneuma* driveth him into the wilderness." The same as verse 10.

Mark 1:23 "There was in their synagogue a man with an *unclean pneuma*," *i.e.*, an evil spirit.

Mark 1:26 " When *the pneuma the unclean*."

The article is used here, only grammatically, in order to identify this *pneuma* with that already mentioned in verse 23.

Mark 1:27 "With authority he commandeth even *the pneumata the unclean*, and they do obey him." Here it is plural, and is used of evil spirits generally.

Mark 2:8 " Jesus perceived in his *pneuma* " : *i.e.*, in Himself. By *Synecdoche*, a part is put for the whole. (See Usage No. IX. above.) The A.V. of 1611 had " S "; but current editions, with R.V., have " s."

Mark 3:11 " And *the pneumata the unclean*, when they saw him, fell down before him," etc. The same as chap. i. 27.

Mark 3:29 " But he that shall blaspheme against *the pneuma the holy* (*i.e.*, the Holy Spirit) hath never for-giveness . . ."

Mark 3:30 "Because they said, He hath an *unclean pneuma*." They said the Lord Jesus was possessed by an evil spirit. This it was that constituted the un-pardonable sin, or blasphemy, against the Holy Spirit, because it was attributing the miracles of Christ to the power of Satan, instead of to God.

Mark 5:2 " There met him out of the tombs a man with an *unclean pneuma*." The same as chap. iii. 30.

Mark 5:8 " Come forth, *the pneuma the unclean*, out of the man." The same as chap. i. 26.

Mark 5:13   " And *the pneumata the unclean* went out,"
etc.   The same as chap. i. 27.

Mark 6:7   " And gave them power (Greek,
authority) over *the pneumata the unclean.*"   The same as
chap. v. 13.

Mark 7:25   " A *certain* woman whose young
daughter had an *unclean pneuma.*"   The same as chap.
v. 2 above.

Mark 8:12   " And he sighed deeply in *the pneuma*
of him": *i.e.*, his spirit.   The same as chap. ii. 8.   Both
versions have " s."

Mark 9:17   " I have brought unto thee my son,
which hath *a dumb pneuma*": *i.e.*, a dumb boy possessed
by an evil spirit.

Mark 9:20   "*The pneuma* tare him."   This passage
furnishes an example showing how the article is
used grammatically.   The article is there.   It is "the
pneuma," but it refers back to the spirit mentioned in
verse 17.

Mark 9:25   " Jesus . . . rebuked *the pneuma the
unclean,* saying unto him, *(The) pneuma the dumb and
deaf,* I charge thee, come out of him."   Here we have,
again, the full expression with two articles used grammatically.

Mark 12:36   " David himself said by *the pneuma the
holy* ": *i.e.*, by the Holy Spirit.   So that it was David's
pen, and David's voice, but they were not David's words.
(See on Matt. xxii. 43, above).   David spake as He was
moved by the Holy Spirit.   To say, therefore, as the
" higher" critics do, that this scripture (Psalm cx. 1)
is not David's at all, is not only to make Christ Himself
a liar, but comes perilously near to blasphemy against
the Holy Spirit.

Mark 13:11   "It is not ye that speak, but *the pneuma the holy*": *i.e.*, the Holy Spirit: *i.e.*, God Himself. (See Matt. x. 20.) The A.V. 1611 had " h "; but the current editions, with R.V., have " H."

Mark 14:38   "*The pneuma* truly *is* ready, but the flesh *is* weak." This is the same as Matt. xxvi. 41.

Mark 15:39   "he gave up his *pneuma*": *i.e.*, he breathed out his *pneuma*, or expired. According to Psalm xxxi. 5, Ecc. xii. 7.

LUKE

Luke 1:15   " He (John) shall be filled with *pneuma hagion** "; *i.e.*, with " power from on high " (ch. xxiv. 49) or with heavenly, Divine and spiritual power. If we take 'Υψίστου (*hupsistou*) here, as a proper name, then we not only may but must use the article " power from the Most High."

Luke 1:17   " He (John) shall go before him (Christ) in [the] *pneuma* and power of Elijah."

Here, the article is not grammatically required after the preposition; its presence is latent, and must be represented according to English Idiom.

The expression "*pneuma* and power" is the Figure *Hendiadys*, by which two nouns are used, but only one is meant; the other becoming a superlative adjective, thus:—" He shall go forth before Him in (the) mighty *pneuma* of Elijah " (with emphasis on the word " mighty "—the mighty spiritual power by which Elijah worked); for *pneuma* already has the idea of power in it (see ch. xxiv. 49, compared with Acts i. 4, 5). What this mighty power was, is seen and defined in the words that follow: " to turn the hearts of the fathers to the

---

*The A.V. and R.V. use capital letters and introduce the definite article.

children, and the disobedient to the wisdom of the just;
to make ready a people prepared for the Lord."

Such a work as this could not be done by any human
power. It would not be inherent in John, nor is it
inherent in any human being. It must come "from on
high." It must be the special, Divine endowment by
the operation of the Holy Spirit of God.* This is seen
in the next example in the case of Mary.

Luke 1:35 "And the angel answered and said to
her, 'Pneuma hagion† shall come upon thee,

> And power of [or from] the Most High shall
> overshadow thee;
> Therefore also that hagion (or, the holy thing) which
> shall be born of thee,
> Shall be called the Son of God.'"

Here, the first two lines are synthetic, the latter
expanding and explaining the former; defining pneuma
hagion (as in ch. xxiv. 49), as being the operation of the
Most High put forth upon her. It is pneuma hagion that
should come upon her, as we have seen above.

Luke 1:41 " Elizabeth was filled with [Greek, of]
pneuma hagion."‡ The verb "filled" goes with this
expression, as we have seen above,§ and the result of
this "filling" is immediately seen in her inspired
utterance (vv. 42-45). Mary's own inspired utterance
was given in direct response to Elizabeth's (see vv.
46-55). It is worthy of note that both these women,
filled with this Divine and spiritual power, acknowledged

---

* We see another illustration of this in the case of Stephen
(Acts vi. 3, 5, 8, 10, and ch. vii.).

† The A.V. and R.V. both use capital letters; and add the definite
article, though there is none in the Greek.

‡ A.V. and R.V. both use capital letters and insert the definite
article.

§ Usage No. XIV., see page 87.

the Deity of Christ. Elizabeth calls Him "my Lord," and Mary says:

Luke 1:47   " My soul ($\psi v \chi \acute{\eta}$) doth magnify the Lord: And my spirit [*pneuma*] hath rejoiced in God my Saviour."

Here, again, the two parallel lines are synthetic; the second expanding and explaining the first.

" My soul," and " my spirit," are both put, by *Synecdoche*, for the whole person (a part being put for the whole). Here, and in all similar expressions, " my soul " means *I myself*.

Whenever this Figure is used instead of the ordinary pronoun, it is for the purpose of putting great emphasis upon it. The ordinary pronoun would be very weak and tame in a case like this.

What Mary says is spoken in immediate response to what Elizabeth had said to her; and the Figure *Synecdoche* gives the emphasis: which may be thus expressed:

" I, even I, do magnify the Lord,
    And I rejoice in Him, my Saviour, God."

In Greek, the pronoun really forms part of the verb. When, therefore, a pronoun is separately expressed and used in addition to the verb, it is very emphatic. But when, as here, instead of even the pronoun we have another noun altogether, turned by this Figure (*Synecdoche*) into a pronoun, it is still more emphatic, and is used to impress us, and to call our attention to the fact.

Luke 1:67   " And his [John's] father Zacharias was filled with (Greek, *of*) *pneuma hagion*, and prophesied."*

Here, the verb " filled " connects the expression with the *operation* of the Holy Spirit; the " gift " in question being the gift of prophecy. The direct result of this

* The A.V. and R.V. again use capital letters, and add the article " the."

filling is seen in the words that follow : "and prophesied, saying " : the inspired utterance being recorded in verses 68-79.

Luke 1:80 " And the child (John) grew, and waxed strong in *pneuma**" (the "in," here, is not the rendering of a preposition, so that the article is not even latent. It is simply the Dative case, and means "as to his *pneuma*."

The word is used here, psychologically, according to Gen. ii. 7. The two parts of human nature are mentioned :

1. As to his body—he grew.
2. As to his *pneuma*—he was strengthened.

Luke 2:25 Of Simeon it is said, " *pneuma hagion*† was upon him "; *i.e.*, power from on high. How this showed itself is immediately explained in the words following :

Luke 2:26 "And it was revealed to him by *the pneuma the holy*, that he should not see death before he had seen the Lord's Christ.

Luke 2:27 " And he came by *the pneuma*‡ into the Temple," &c.

In these three verses we have—

(1) The statement (*v.* 25) that Simeon had *pneuma hagion* "upon him "; *i.e.*, not the Holy Spirit, but His powerful operation ; not the Giver, but His gift.

(2) Then we have the statement (*v.* 26) that the Giver of this wondrous gift was the Holy Spirit. He it was who " revealed " to Simeon the fact stated.

---

* Both A.V. and R.V. use a small " s.''

† Both A.V. and R.V. use capital letters and arbitrarily add the definite article.

‡ The A.V. of 1611, had " s.'' But current editions, with R.V., have " S.''

(3) That through the power of this *pneuma* he came into the Temple (*v.* 27). The article here grammatically identifies this *pneuma* with the person just mentioned in the previous verse (*v.* 26). And, though the preposition (ἐν, *en, by* or *through*) is used, the article is added for the purpose of ensuring this identification (*v.* 27).

(4) We have in verses 29-32 Simeon's inspired utterance—the gift of " speaking " which was the manifestation of the *pneuma hagion* which was upon him.

Luke 2:40   All the Textual Critics (Lachmann, Tischendorf, Tregelles, Alford, Westcott and Hort, and the Revised Version) omit the word πνεύματι (*pneumati*) " *in* (or, as to his) *pneuma*." This is the first passage from which, according to the Critical Greek Texts, *pneuma* is to be omitted.

Luke 3:16   " He (Christ) shall baptize you with *pneuma hagion** and fire." The same as Matt. iii. 11.

Luke 3:22   " *The pneuma the holy*, descended." See Matt. iii. 16.

Luke 4:1   (twice). " And Jesus being full of *pneuma hagion†* returned from the Jordan, and was led by *the pneuma†* into the wilderness." Here, *pneuma* is used twice : first of the gift, then of the Giver. The expression *pneuma hagion* (having no article) refers to the Divine " power from on high " with which He was filled by the operation of the Holy Spirit ; while in the latter expression, the Filler is emphasised by the presence of the article (" the ") which is used with *pneuma*, though the grammar does not require it after the preposition (ἐν, *en, by*).

---

* The A.V. and R.V. both use capitals and add the definite article.

† The A.V. of 1611 had a small " s " for the latter word ; but current editions, with the R.V., use capitals in both cases.

Luke 4:14   "Jesus returned, in the power *of the pneuma*, into Galilee."

Here the article is used in the Greek (though it is not necessary after the preposition (ἐν, *en*, *in*); except for the purpose of emphasis, and in order to identify *pneuma* with the Giver of the power. The Genitive is that of *origin*, marking the source of the power.

Luke 4:18   " He found the place where it was written, *pneuma**** from the Lord (or Jehovah's *pneuma*) is upon me, because he hath anointed me to preach the Gopel to the poor," etc.   What this *pneuma* was we are immediately told.   It was the Divine *power* of Adonai Jehovah (Is. lxi. 1, etc.), as manifested in His preaching to the poor, healing the broken-hearted, liberating Satan's captives, giving sight to the blind, etc.

It is called "*pneuma* from the Lord " here, for the purpose of identifying this with the *pneuma hagion* received by Christ according to the prophecy of Isaiah, which was that day " fulfilled in their ears."

Luke 4:33   " And in the synagogue there was a man that had a *pneuma* of an unclean demon."

Here it is the Genitive of apposition ; " the *pneuma* (that is to say) an unclean demon.   It does not mean that the demon had a *pneuma*, but that he was a *pneuma*. It might be rendered "a spirit which was an unclean demon."

Luke 4 :36   "With authority and power he com- mandeth *the* unclean *pneumata*, and they came out."

Luke 6:18   "And they that were vexed with unclean *pneumata* .   .   .   were healed."

---

* Both versions insert the article in accordance with the requirements of English Idiom, and use " S."

Luke 7:21   " He cured many of their infirmities and plagues, and of evil *pneumata*."

Luke 8:2   The same as ch. vii. 21.

Luke 8:29   " For he had commanded *the pneuma the unclean* to come out of the man."

This case is remarkable; for the construction is the same as the fullest form used for denoting the Holy Spirit Himself. He is " *the pneuma* the holy." This is " *the pneuma* the unclean." This is to emphasise the importance of this particular case. In verse 27 we are told that the man was possessed with " demons." And, indeed, " he said " his name was " Legion, because many demons were entered into him."

It is worthy of note that all the so-called " spirits " with whom the so-called " spiritualists " have dealings must be these evil and unclean spirits, or demons. For we never read of good *pneumata* having dealings with mankind. And the *pneumata* of dead men cannot have such dealings with the living : for they all alike return to God (Ecc. xii. 7.   Ps. xxxi. 5.   Luke xxiii. 46.   Acts vii. 59).   He is not only the giver of the *pneuma*, but He is the custodian of all *pneumata* after death (see Num. xvi. 22 ; xxvii. 16.   Zech. xii. 1.   Heb. xii. 9).   Now, they are imperfect ; but in resurrection they will be " made perfect " (Heb. xi. 28).   God being their custodian, they can have no communication with mankind.   God forbade this communication while they were alive, and He is not going to allow it after this life.   It follows therefore that the spirits of " Spiritualism " are evil and unclean demons.

Luke 8:55   " And straightway her *pneuma** came again."   The usage here is psychological ; and is in accordance with Gen. ii. 7.   Zech. xii. 1.

* Both A.V. and R.V. have " s " here.

Luke 9:39   "Lo, *a pneuma* taketh him": *i.e.*, an evil *pneuma;* for he is called a "demon" in verse 42 : "the demon threw him down."

Luke 9:42   "Jesus rebuked *the pneuma the unclean.*"   Here the articles are grammatical (as in ch. viii. 29) for the purpose of emphasis, and for identifying it with the *pneuma* of verse 39.

Luke 9:55   All the Critical Greek Texts and R.V. omit the words from "and said" down to (and including) the words "to save them."   This is the second passage where *pneuma* is to be omitted, and if so it calls for no further explanation.   The two verses read, "But he turned and rebuked them.   And they went to another village."

It is supposed that a later scribe ventured to supply what the Lord said.   At first, probably, it was only put as a gloss in the margin; and then some other transcriber afterwards, taking it to be the indication of an omission, put in into the text.

Luke 10:20   "Rejoice not that *the pneumata* are subject unto you; but rather rejoice, because your names are written in Heaven."

Here the plural is used of evil spirits or demons.

Luke 10:21   All the Critical Texts and R.V. add the preposition ἐν (*en*) *by*; also the words τῷ ἁγίῳ (*tō hagiō*) *the holy*.   The passage therefore reads, "Jesus rejoiced by the *pneuma the holy* * ": *i.e.*, by the power of the Holy Spirit.   This full expression emphasises the fact that it was the Holy Spirit, the Great Giver of the joy, as well as the power over all unclean spirits and demons,

---

* The A.V. has a small "s." The R.V. reads "in the Holy Spirit."

Hence it is that the fact of attributing this power put forth by Christ to the work of Beelzebub is blasphemy against the Holy Spirit.

Luke 11:13   "If ye then, being evil, know how to give good gifts unto your children ; how much more shall your heavenly Father give *pneuma hagion*† to them that ask Him."

There are four contrasts in this verse.

- (1) Earth and heaven: for "heaven" is in the singular, and the contrast therefore is with the earth: we might render it "[that giveth gifts] out of heaven."

- (2) Human, and therefore evil,‡ parents, in contrast with God our Father.

- (3) The children of these human parents, in contrast with the children of God.

- (4) The gift of temporal things, in contrast with the bestowal of spiritual gifts.

Parts of the "Sermon on the Mount" recorded in Matt. v.—vii., were *repeated* at different times and on subsequent occasions, as recorded in Luke.   In Matthew it was spoken as a connected whole before the calling of the Twelve ; but this repetition of Matt. vii. 9-11 here, in Luke xi. 10-13, was after the calling of the Twelve and of the Seventy.

In Matt. vii. 11, He says, "How much more shall your Father which is in heaven give good things to them that ask Him ?" But when He repeats it in Luke xi. 13 He varies it by saying "*pneuma hagion*" instead of

† Both A.V. and R.V. use capital letters and insert the article, though there is none in the Greek.

‡ πονηρός (*ponēros*) *evil* in nature.   The verb is ὑπάρχοντες (*huparchontes*) *existing: i.e., being evil* to begin with.

" good things." By this he shows that *pneuma hagion* is the same as " good things "; except that in Matthew they include *temporal* things, while in Luke He confines the " good things " to *spiritual gifts*.

This passage, therefore, does not mean that unconverted people are to pray for the Holy Spirit (as the insertion of the article and the use of the capital "S" in A.V. and R.V. imply), but that the children of God (who can pray only by the operation of the Holy Spirit) are to ask their heavenly Father to give them spiritual gifts or " power from on high."

The argument is that if earthly parents, who by nature are evil, give good gifts to their children, how much more shall our heavenly Father, who is goodness itself, give infinitely better things to His children; yea, He blesses them with " all spiritual blessings " in Christ.

We thus see how the expression *pneuma hagion* includes all good gifts, whereas any other expression would limit the blessing to some special gift.

Luke 11:24,25 " When *the unclean pneuma* is gone out of a man, he walketh through dry* places, seeking rest ;† and, finding none, he saith, I will return unto MY HOUSE whence I CAME OUT; and when he cometh he findeth it swept and garnished."

Luke 11:26 " Then goeth he and taketh to him seven other *pneumata* more wicked than himself, and they enter in and DWELL there ;‡ and the last state of that man is worse than the first."

Here the Lord repeats what He had said in Matt. xii.

---

* ἀνύδρων (anudrōn) *waterless*.

† ἀνάπαυσις (anapausis) *temporary rest;* in contrast with κατάπαυσις (katapausis) *complete rest*.

‡ κατοικέω (katoikeo) *to settle down*, or, *take up one's abode*.

43-45; when he concluded His parable by giving its interpretation :—" Even so shall it be also unto (or, with) this wicked generation" (or nation).

The Lord taught, by this parable, that the nation of Israel was meant by the man possessed of an evil spirit : and, instigated by it, the nation rejected Christ. But that spirit went out of its own accord, and by and by it will return in the perfection of evil spiritual power. It will find the nation reformed, and outwardly " swept and garnished ;" and the last state of that wicked nation shall be worse than the first.

They rejected Christ, who came in His Father's name. They will receive Anti-christ, who will come in his own name (John v. 43). THE* strong man will be in possession : he will be keeping his palace : his goods will be in peace (Dan. xi. 21. 1 Thess. v. 3); when the " stronger than he shall come upon him, and overcome him," and shall " divide his spoils."

Never more will he return, for he will be "cast out" (and not merely go out, of his own accord).

That is how it will be with the nation of Israel. It will be " even so." This is the *interpretation* of the parable; but, there is an *application* to this *present* generation. When the evil spirit " is gone out of a man " of his own accord, and the efforts of a professing world succeed in making him "a reformed character," then the evil spirit returns in seven-fold power, and the last state of that man is worse than the first.

Only when the evil spirit "in possession"—"the strong man "—is " CAST OUT " by the stronger than he, then he never can return ; and the man will enjoy an everlasting peace and security (Ps. lxxii. 3, 7. Isa. ii. 4).

---

* The article is emphatic in Luke xi. 21 and Matt. xii. 29.

Luke 12:10 he " that blasphemeth against *the holy pneuma*": *i.e.*, the Holy Spirit, as in Matt. xii. 31.

Luke 12:12 The same as verse 10.

Luke 13:11 " There was a woman which had *a pneuma* of infirmity": this may have been a demon, causing peculiar sickness or suffering: but the case is a remarkable one. The woman is said to have been unable to straighten herself upright. The negative is μή (*mē*), not οὐ (*ou*) ; and is therefore subjective. She *felt as if* she could not do so. And the Lord is not said to have bidden any spirit to depart out of her; but He calls her " a daughter of Abraham," and He says " Satan had bound her." It appears, therefore, to have been a *nervous disorder ;* and had to do with her *pneuma.*

Luke 23:46 " Father, into thy hands I commend my *pneuma*."* The usage here is psychological, according to Gen. ii. 7. Ps. xxxi. 5. Ecc. xii. 7; and Acts vii. 59.

Luke 24:37 "they supposed that they had seen *a pneuma†*": *i.e.*, an angel, or spiritual being; not the spirit of a dead man, for that cannot be seen, having returned to God who gave it. This the Lord explains to them in verse 39 (see below).

Luke 24:39 " Behold my hands and my feet, that it is I myself: handle me, and see; for *a pneuma* hath not flesh and bones, as ye see me have."

This tells us that the resurrection body, though called a *pneuma* (or spiritual) body in 1 Cor. xv. 44-46 (see above, under Usage XIII.), will not be exactly the same as that of the angels. They were created *pneumata*, or purely spiritual beings. We are created *human* beings

---

* The A.V. and R.V. both have " s."

† The A.V. and R.V. both have " s."

having a *pneuma*. In resurrection we shall be *pneumatika*, but of a different order from that of angels and demons. They never had, and will not have, flesh and bones, as we shall have, for we shall be like our risen Lord (Phil. iii. 21). His was made a *pneuma*-body in resurrection (1 Cor. xv. 45. 1 Pet. iii. 18). Even so will ours be made, when, like Him, we shall be raised from the dead (1 Cor. xv. 44).

JOHN

John 1:32 "I saw *the pneuma* descending from heaven." The same as Mark i. 10. Compare Matt. iii. 16.

John 1:33 (twice). "Upon whom thou shalt see *the pneuma* descending, and remaining on him, the same is he which baptizeth with *pneuma hagion*."*

In the first instance, we have (from the context and the definite article) the Holy Spirit; and in the second, we have His spiritual power, or spiritual gifts, as the medium with which He (Christ) would baptize, as opposed to the material medium (water) with which John had baptized.† In the former we have the Giver, and in the latter we have the gifts which he gives.

In Acts xi. 17 it is actually called "the Gift," and is thus distinguished from the Giver.

It is important for us to note this remarkable contrast between the baptism of John and of Christ. Seven times‡ our attention is distinctly called to the important contrast between the two baptisms and the two opposite mediums which John and Christ would use. One was

---

* The A.V. and R.V. insert the article and use capital letters.

† We have shown above, under *Usage* No. XIV., that *pneuma*, when mentioned in connection with baptism, is always called *pneuma hagion*.

‡ Matt. iii. 11. Mark i. 8. Luke iii. 16. John i. 26-33. Acts i. 5; xi. 15, 16; xix. 4.

material, the other was to be *spiritual* (Eph. iv. 5); one was "water," the other was *pneuma*. Compare the passage (John iii. 5 below), where this medium is called "spiritual water," the emphasis being put on the word "spiritual."

John 3:5 "Verily, verily I say unto thee, except a man be born* of water and *pneuma*, he cannot enter into the kingdom of God."

In the A.V. of 1611, the translators inserted the article, but used a small "s."† In the current editions of the A.V., and in the R.V., we have the article and a capital "S." The question for us to answer is: Which of these is correct? A difficulty is created for the English reader by this alteration: and he is not only entitled to ask, but bound to find out, which of these two is correct: the A.V. of 1611, or the A.V. as printed to-day in the current editions. It is our duty to place all the data before him that he may be able to judge for himself.

(1) Note that the words were spoken to an Israelite, to a Ruler, a Pharisee, and a "Master in Israel" who ought to have known, from the Old Testament, the truth which the Lord was here enunciating: "Verily, verily, I say unto THEE."

(2) It was spoken about the "KINGDOM," and has therefore nothing whatever to do with the "Church of God." The words referred to "earthly things," as the Lord Himself stated in verse 12.

(3) Nicodemus ought to have known and understood what the Lord was teaching: seeing it had been clearly foretold, that, when Israel should be restored and brought back to the Land, and the kingdom set up, everything was to be changed from the material to the spiritual. Their

---

* Greek, *begotten*.
† According to the reprint in the R.V.

"heart of flesh" was to be taken away, and a new heart was to be substituted for it. Israel was to be cleansed and purified, and therefore "water" is used as the symbol. See Ezek. xxxvi. 24-30; xxxvii. 9: and compare Num. xix. 9, 13. Lev. xiv 6-9. Zech. xiii. 1 (with xii. 9-14).

But before this spiritual *water* could "cleanse," spiritual *fire* was to "purge." The refiner's fire was to purify (Matt. iii. 11). This refining (or baptism of "*pneuma* and fire") is described in Mal. iii. 1-6; iv. 1, and would be in judgment.

In Isa. iv. 4, these two baptisms are mentioned together, in connection with that future day "when the Lord shall have washed away the filth of the daughters of Zion, and shall have purged the blood of Jerusalem from the midst thereof by the spirit of judgment, and by the spirit of burning." This purging is the spiritual fire of Mal. iv. 1, and Matt. iii. 11.

But Israel is also to be cleansed and purified, as well as purged and refined; and the *spiritual water* of John iii. 5 is used as the symbol of this "washing away" of Isa. iv. 4.

It is the spiritual water of Ezek. xxxvi. 24-30 and John iii. 5: and is to "wash away the filth of the daughters of Zion." Compare Isa. xliv. 3, and Zech. xiii. 1.

These are the scriptures which should have explained the Lord's words to Nicodemus; and which should now explain them to us.

If the church insists on having the "the water" of John iii. 5, it must also have "the fire" of Matt. iii. 11. But here, as in the Prophets, the church picks and chooses, taking the blessings for itself, and leaving the curses and judgments for Israel.

The holiest among us appropriate the "water" of

Ezekiel xxxvi., but carefully leave the " fire " of Malachi iv.; though both are so identified with Israel, that it seems wonderful that such "discriminating" selection could ever have been made.

(4) In order to take John iii. 5, which is spoken of the " Kingdom," and to secure it for the church, the definite article (which is absent from the Greek) is inserted in the English, and a Figure of Speech (*Hendiadys*) is taken *literally* by those who make war with the church of Rome for doing the very same thing, when it takes another Figure *(Metaphor)* literally : " This is my body."

Both are Figures of Speech ; the one as much as the other : and two gigantic errors connected with the two Sacraments have been built up upon them, by taking them literally : Baptismal Regeneration, and Transub-stantiation.

Romanists are more consistent in this than Protestants : for they do treat *both* passages in the *same* way, but Protestants, with great inconsistency, take John iii. 5 literally ; and will not allow Romanists to take Matt. xxvi. 26 literally ; while Romanists persist in taking both passages literally, agreeing with those Protestants who treat John iii 5, in such a way that it is made the basis of the doctrine of Baptismal Regeneration.

Seeing that these two errors have desolated the church, and been the fountain head of all the corruptions which are leading up to and will soon end in the great Apostasy, does it not behove us to look carefully at this corrupt root from which comes the corrupt fruit of both these deadly errors ?

First, then, there is no article in the Greek, either with the word "water," or the word " spirit." It reads " ἐξ ὕδατος καὶ πνεύματος (*ex hudatos kai pneumatos*) *of water and pneuma.* It is the Figure *Hendiadys* (as

Matt. xxvi. 26 is the Figure *Metaphor**) by which, though two words are used, only one thing is meant.† Here the one thing is "water:" but the Lord emphasises the fact that this water is not to be *material* as it was under the law, but *spiritual* as stated in Ezek. xxxvi. The Figure is best represented idiomatically in English thus: "Except a man be born of water, yea, *spiritual water*."

What this spiritual water is to be is explained in John vii. 39 (see below). It is *pneuma* : which was not, and could not be, then given, the Lord Jesus being not yet glorified.

(5) There are three great reasons why these words cannot be interpreted of the church of God in this present dispensation.

(*a*) The *time* referred to in Ezek. xxxvi. 24, 25, for the fulfilment of that prophecy is the time of Israel's restoration to their Land.

"I will take you from among the heathen,
And gather you out of all countries,
And will bring you into your own LAND.
THEN will I sprinkle clean water upon you,
and ye shall be clean :
From all your filthiness, and from all your idols,
will I cleanse you."

(*b*) The other reason is given in the next verses (26, 27).

---

* See Figures of Speech, pages 664, 738, and a small pamphlet, "This is my Body" (one penny), both by the same author, and published by Eyre and Spottiswoode, 33 Paternoster Row, London.

† As in Acts xiii. 13, "oxen and garlands" means "garlanded oxen" and therefore ready for heathen sacrifice. 2 Sam. xx. 19, "a city and a mother." *i.e.*, a mother city, or a metropolitan city.

" A new heart also will I give you,
And a new spirit will I put within you :
And I will take away the stony heart out of your
    flesh,
And I will give you an heart of flesh.
And I will put my spirit within you,
And cause you to walk in my statutes,
And ye shall keep my judgments, and do them."

(c) The consequent blessings are to be material, as well as spiritual (verses 28-31, and 33-36).

" And ye shall dwell in the land that I gave to
    your fathers ;
And ye shall be my people and I will be your
    God.

I will also save you from all your uncleannesses:
And I will call for the corn, and will increase it,
And lay no famine upon you.
And I will multiply the fruit of the tree, and the
    increase of the field,
That ye shall receive no more reproach of famine
    among the heathen.

THEN shall ye remember your own evil ways,
And your doings that were not good,
And shall lothe yourselves in your own sight
For your iniquities and for your abominations . . .
Thus saith Adonai Jehovah ;

IN THE DAY when I shall have cleansed you
    from all your iniquities
I will also cause you to DWELL IN THE
    CITIES,
And the wastes shall be builded.

And the desolate land shall be tilled,
Whereas it lay desolate in the sight of all that
    passed by.

> And they shall say, THIS LAND that was
> desolate
> Is become like the garden of Eden :
> And the waste and desolate and ruined cities
> Are become fenced, and are inhabited.
> THEN the heathen that are left round about you,
> Shall know that I the LORD build the ruined
> places,
> And plant that that was desolate :
> I the LORD have spoken it,
> And I will do it."

It must be clear to all who desire rightly to divide "the word of truth" that these Scriptures cannot be interpreted of the church of God in this present dispensation. The Lord Jesus distinctly told Nicodemus that, as "a master in Israel," he ought to have known them, for they related to "earthly things."

On the other hand, the church's standing is entirely "heavenly" and spiritual. The old heart is neither "changed" (according to popular phraseology), nor is it "taken away" or eradicated (according to popular theology). The new nature which cannot sin is given to the believer ; but the old nature which cannot but sin remains as long as we are in this mortal body. Not to know this is to be ignorant of the fundamental Christian position and teaching as set forth in Rom. i.-viii.

Israel, when restored, will have an indefectible nature. The child of God will not possess his until he is delivered, as he, one day, will be, "thank God" (the Apostle says), either by translation, or resurrection.

John 3:6   (twice). "That which is born of *the pneuma* is *pneuma*."

It is a question, whether, here, *the pneuma* does not mean more than the Holy Spirit, and denote God

Himself. It is the assertion of a great eternal principle, that whatever is begotten by God is Divine. Hence that new nature which is begotten in us makes us "partakers of the Divine nature." It is Divine, and therefore perfect, and cannot sin. In any case, we have in the first *pneuma*, (with the article), the Holy Spirit, or God ; and, in the second, that which is begotten of or produced by Him in us, whether the new nature, or spiritual gifts, or "power from on high."

The A.V. of 1611 had a "s" in both cases,* but current editions, with R.V., now print the former with "S" and the latter with "s."

We have, here, "the teaching of Jesus"; but those who love to call it thus will not have it. Popular teaching, to-day, is all based on the principle that the flesh can be improved : whereas the Lord declares that "that which is born of the flesh, is flesh" (and remains flesh); and "that which is born of the spirit, is spirit" (and remains spirit). There is no process by which the flesh can be changed into spirit. This is the great fundamental truth of Christianity. Christianity is the formation of Christ (the *pneuma Christou*, Rom. viii. 9) within the believer (Gal. iv. 19. Col. i. 27), by the Spirit of God ; and this is *pneuma*, and is Divine. But all "Religion" consists in the improvement of the flesh. It is all external. It all has to do with "that which goeth into the mouth" (Matt. xv. 16-20. Mark vii. 18-23). The one is Divine : the other is human. The one is eternal : the other is only for time.

John 3:8   This verse exhibits a beautiful Figure of Speech called *Epanadiplosis* (or *Encircling*) : by which an important pronouncement is emphasised, by being rounded off, so to speak, and made a complete and

---

* According to the reprint in the R.V.

independent statement, by commencing and finishing with the same word, or words : the words, here, being "*the pneuma*."*

The use of this Figure is to mark the passage as being very weighty : making it to stand out so clearly that it may attract our attention, and cause us to consider the solemnity, significance, and importance of its statement.

This passage is part of a revelation concerning the Holy Spirit and His work. And the Figure, not being heeded by the A.V. and R.V., requires to be presented in a new translation. The first *pneuma* in this verse is translated "wind" in both versions, though this is the only place, out of the 385 occurrences, where it is so rendered. If "wind" had been meant there is its own proper noun which could have been used, *viz.*, ἄνεμος *(anemos)*.†

John uses this word ἄνεμος *(anemos)* when he wishes to express *wind* in ch. vi. 18 ; and would, without doubt, have used it here if *wind* had been meant.

The verse consistently rendered will stand thus :—

"THE PNEUMA breatheth where He willeth, and His voice thou hearest ; but thou knowest not‡ whence He cometh and whither He goeth. Thus it is [with] everyone who has been begotten by THE PNEUMA."

---

* See *Figures of Speech*, published by Messrs. Eyre & Spottiswoode, 33 Paternoster Row, London, pp. 245-249, where many examples are given : *e.g.*, Ps. liii. 2. Mark xiii. 35-37. Luke xii. 5. Gal. ii. 20 (Greek). Phil. iv. 4, etc.

† It occurs 31 times, and is always rendered *wind*: *viz.*, Matt. vii. 25, 27 ; viii. 26, 27 ; xi. 7 ; xiv. 24, 30, 32 ; xxiv. 31. Mark iv. 37, 39 (twice), 41 ; vi. 48, 51 ; xiii. 27. Luke vii. 24 ; viii. 23, 24, 25. John vi. 18. Acts xxvii. 4, 7, 14, 15. Eph. iv. 14. James iii. 4. Jude 12. Rev. vi. 13 ; vii. 1 (twice).

‡ The word for innate or intuitive knowledge ; and the negative for a categorical denial of the fact.

The Spirit moves, as in the old creation (Gen. i. 2). The subjects of His new creation-work hear His voice, and feel His power; but they cannot tell whence He cometh, or whither He goeth. As there, He commanded the light to shine out of darkness, so now He causes Divine light, " the light of the knowledge of the glory of God," to shine in our hearts, by revealing God to us in the person of Jesus Christ. Compare 2 Cor. iv. 6, and v. 17, 18.

It cannot mean " the wind," for the wind has no will. But the Spirit has a will and a voice, and it is of Him that the new nature is begotten.

The verb θέλειν (*thelein*), *to will*, occurs 213 times; and expresses a personal act, or desire, or determination, proceeding from one capable of wishing, willing, or determining. See the nearly synonymous expression in 1 Cor. xii. 11—"But all these worketh that one and the self-same Spirit, dividing to every man, severally as HE WILL."*

Moreover, it is not correct to assert this of the " wind." We *do* know whence it comes, and whither it goes: and the Scriptures affirm that the comings and goings of the wind can be known and traced (see Job i. 19. Eccles. i. 6. Ezek. xxxvii. 9). But not so of the spirit (see Eccles. xi. 5), where " spirit " is placed in direct contrast with " wind" which is mentioned in the previous verse, and not in likeness to it.

The context shows that the things contrasted are " flesh " and " spirit," earthly things and heavenly things. And AS the Spirit in His movements is contrary to nature and above nature (*i.e.*, super-natural), SO is that which is begotten of the Spirit. Those who are thus twice born are " sons of God " by the second

---

* But here the word is βούλεται (*bouletai*), and refers to *counsel* rather than *determination*.

birth. Therefore the world (the once born) knoweth us not, because it knew Him not (1 John iii. 1). As the world knoweth not the motions of the Spirit of God, so the motions of the *pneuma* within us—the new breathings, the new will, and the new desires of the new nature in those who are begotten of *the pneuma*—are also unknown.

John 3:34 " He giveth not *the pneuma* by measure unto him."

This clause evidently presented difficulties to the Transcribers of the Text; and it seems as though they added ὁ Θεός (*ho theos*) *God*: for it is put in brackets by Lachmann and Tregelles; while Tischendorf, Alford, Westcott and Hort, and R.V. omit it altogether. The Revisers render it "for he giveth not the Spirit by measure."

The article with *pneuma* seems to mark it as the subject of the verb " giveth " and not the object; just as it marks "God" as the subject in the previous clause (" God is true.) "

The rendering therefore may be " For not (with emphasis on the " not," standing as it does, by *Hyperbaton*, at the beginning of the sentence) by measure doth the *Pneuma* (*i.e.*, the Holy Spirit) give [the words of God] *unto him*." As there is no object mentioned after the verb "giveth," and as (being transitive) it must have an object, we have supplied (from the previous clause) " the words of God." The A.V. rightly supplies the other *Ellipsis* with the words " *unto him*."

The meaning of the whole verse, therefore, is, that " He whom God hath sent speaketh the words of God : for the Spirit giveth not the words of God by measure unto him."

Hence *pneuma*, here, having the article, denotes the

Giver, and not the gift: and the gift that He gave to Christ was not Himself, but "the words of God," which Christ was claiming to speak, because He was sent by God. This we can understand. But how a Person can be given by measure; or how the First Person can give the Third Person to the Second; or how the Third Person can give Himself to the Second baffles all comprehension; besides introducing a difficulty into the passage which is not there.

John 4:23 "The hour cometh, and now is, when the true worshippers shall worship the Father in *pneuma* and truth."

Here, we have the Figure *Hendiadys* again, as in ch. iii. 5. There are no articles in either passage. Yet both versions arbitrarily insert the article in ch. iii. 5, and put a capital "S," rendering it "the Spirit"; while, in ch. iv. 23, where the conditions are exactly the same, they do not use the article, and put a small "s." The A.V. says "in spirit and in truth." The R.V. says "in spirit and truth." The latter is more correct; for the word "in" is used only once in the Greek; showing that only one thing is meant, though two words are used.

In chap. iii. 5 we have "water and *pneuma*"; in ch. iv. 23 we have "*pneuma* and truth." The second noun becomes the superlative adjective in each case. In the the former it is "spiritual water"; in this it is "true spirit."

We have the same Figure repeated in the next verse.

John 4:24 (twice). "God is *pneuma*": not, as in A.V., "God is a Spirit;" but as in R.V. margin, "God is spirit." Here the definite article is used with "God," marking the noun, which is to be taken as the subject of the verb (as it marks *pneuma* in ch. iii. 34); otherwise it would be "the Spirit is God." But here, it says

" God is *pneuma* "; This is a unique and special usage of the word *pneuma*, which shows that it is not always used in precisely the same sense; and should prepare us for the special study of each passage where it occurs, with the view of discovering the *use* of the word in the Greek, and the *usage* of the word as to its signification.

Then we have a repetition of the statement made in the previous verse: "and they that worship Him must worship Him in *pneuma* and truth": *i.e.*: in true spirit, or truly in spirit, or truly with the spirit: *i.e.*: with those spiritual powers and gifts which He gives.

There is no article; and it is not the Holy Spirit who is meant. *Pneuma* is used psychologically of human nature: and we are taught that true worship cannot be offered with the " flesh," or with our bodies, or with any or all of our senses. It must be truly spiritual: *i.e.*: with our spirit; or it will be fleshly or sensuous worship rendered with our senses. There is no *choice* left us in the matter. It is useless for us to say " I *like* this in worship," or "I *prefer* this." The great rubric, that overrides all man's rubrics, declares that they that worship God, who is *pneuma*, MUST worship Him truly with their *pneuma*. This "must" is the same as the " must " in John iii. 7: "Ye MUST be born again ": *i.e.*: of spiritual water. It is the same as ch. iii. 14: " Even so MUST the Son of Man be lifted up."

The statement, here, with regard to the "true worshippers " is, that they cannot worship except with the innermost occupation of their heart. No outward act of the body, in kneeling or standing, singing or saying, gazing or listening, eating or drinking, can be substituted for that which MUST be *spiritual*.

All that does not conduce to this end is not only a hindrance to true worship, but is positively destructive of it. To do anything that attracts or distracts our minds or thoughts, or any of our senses, is a snare of the devil, making it impossible for us to render the only worship which the Father seeks and accepts.

It is this which marks off true worship from false, from the very beginning, in the oldest lesson which is given and written on the very forefront of revelation (Gen. iv.). Abel, in the obedience of faith, worshipped God, as He must have commanded; for he worshipped "by faith," and "faith cometh by hearing." Cain worshipped according to his own invention; he "brought of the fruit of the ground"; of which the LORD God had said (ch. iii. 17), "Cursed is the ground." "The way of Cain" (Jude 11) was, therefore, to offer to God, in worship, that which He had put under the curse.

The flesh is under the curse. It has no place in Divine worship. True worshippers are they who "worship God in spirit, ... and have no confidence in the flesh" (Phil. iii. 3): "The flesh profiteth nothing" (John. vi. 63).

Sensuous worship : *i.e.* : any worship which is the effort of the flesh, or any of our senses; is a direct insult to God; and is that to which He will "not have respect." It must be an abomination in His sight.

To put up anything to be looked at; to perform anything to be listened to; to burn anything to be smelt; to do anything to be admired and make the people say "How beautiful!" is not true worship. It may be called so, it may bear any name that men may be pleased to give it, but it is not what is here defined as the worship which God "seeketh," or as the worship which "must" be rendered by the "true worshippers."

Those who make so much of what they call "the teaching of Jesus" would do well to read, mark, learn, study, and obey this, which is *His teaching* concerning true worship.

Then, when the seed, the word of God, has been sown in the heart and received by "them that hear," no organ would be allowed to crash in with some march or fugue; and thus illustrate and prove the truth of the Saviour's words: "Then cometh the devil, and taketh away the word out of their hearts, lest they should believe and be saved" (Luke viii. 11, 12).

No! "God is *pneuma*: and they that worship Him MUST worship Him in true *pneuma*": *i.e.*, with those spiritual powers which are His gift only, and of His operation alone.

When we consider the burden of the flesh, and how difficult it makes the effort to fix and occupy the heart with God without a wandering thought, we see that it is a sin of no ordinary kind, and a snare of no ordinary subtlety, to do anything to increase that difficulty by attracting or distracting our thoughts, or any of our senses; thus helping, and actually causing, the thoughts to wander from Him, who "must" be alone the one and only object before our hearts.

When one can be found who has ever said the "Lord's Prayer" through without a wandering thought, let him be the one to cast the first stone at what is here said; or, let him and all others hold their peace and tremble before this solemn utterance of the Lord Jesus Christ.

John 6:63 (twice). "It is *the pneuma* that quickeneth; the flesh profiteth nothing: the words that I speak unto you, they are *pneuma*,* and they are life."

Here, with the first *pneuma*, the definite article is used, not to denote the Holy Spirit, but grammatically.

It is used psychologically according to Gen. ii. 7. Man was made "flesh" out of the dust of the ground;

---

* The A.V. of 1611 used "S" in both cases; but the current editions, with R.V., have "s."

and was only "flesh" until the quickening "*pneuma*" was breathed into his nostrils; then he "became a living soul." At death *the pneuma* returns to God, and is commended to Him (Ps. xxxi. 5. Luke xxiii. 46. Acts vii. 59). It "RE-turns to God who gave it" (Ecc. xii. 7): for "God is *pneuma*," and He is the custodian of all *pneumata* (Num. xvi. 22; xxvii. 16).

"The body without *pneuma* is dead" (Jas. ii. 26). So man, when the *pneuma* returns to God who gave it, is dead, and he who was before called "a living soul" is called a "dead soul." (See Lev. xxi. 11. Num. vi. 6, and compare Num. ix. 6, 7, 10; xix. 11, 13. It is also used of the "dead" in Lev. xxii. 4. Hag. ii. 13).

The Hebrew word *Nephesh (soul)* being translated "body" in these passages, hides this psychological truth from the English reader. Neither in the A.V. nor in the R.V. is there even a marginal note to inform the reader of this important fact.

The teaching of the Lord Jesus (John vi. 63) is that, as the flesh without the *pneuma* is dead, so "words" are useless and are dead without *pneuma*; but HIS words are *pneuma*, and therefore "life" and life-giving. They give life to those who are dead in sins, just as the *pneuma* gave life to Adam's flesh; and as works manifest the presence of living faith which is "faith of the operation of God." (Compare with this, 2 Cor. iii. 6, 17 below; and Jas. ii. 26).

John 7:39 (twice). "This spake he of *the pneuma,* which they that believe on him should (ἔμελλον, *emellon, were about to*) receive: for *pneuma** was not yet given, because Jesus was not yet glorified."

The fact that the second time *pneuma* occurs in this verse it is without the article (though both the A.V. and

---

* Or *pneuma hagion.* Tregelles and Alford put "holy" within brackets, and the R.V. puts it in the margin.

R.V. insert it), and that it is spoken of as not being given until after the Lord Jesus was glorified, shows that it is the gift, and not the Giver, that is the subject of this verse. The Holy Spirit is the Giver of the gift.

The gift He had spoken of was that, out of "the belly" of the believer should flow "living water." "Belly" is here put by *Metonymy* (of the subject) for the inward parts (mind, heart, thoughts, feeling, etc.)*

It is difficult to understand how the Holy Spirit can "flow forth" from every individual believer, seeing there is only one Holy Spirit and many believers. But His gifts and graces and powers, produced by His operations within. When *these* are given, they can "flow forth" and be manifested in life and blessing, as living water conveys blessing and refreshment whither it goes.

John 11:33   "Jesus . . . groaned in *the pneuma* [of him] "; or, in his *pneuma*.† Here, *pneuma* is put by *Synecdoche* for himself. Compare chap. vi. 61, where we have "in himself" without the Figure *Synecdoche*.

John 13:21   The same as ch. xi. 33. Here both A.V. and R.V. have "s," in ch. xi. 33.

John 14:17   "*The pneuma* of truth." Here, the article and the context show that the Holy Spirit is spoken of as the source and the Giver of truth.

John 14:26   "The Comforter, [which is] *the pneuma the holy*." This full expression signifies the Holy Spirit.

John 15:26   "The *pneuma* of truth": *i.e.*: the Holy Spirit is the source of all truth, as in ch. xiv. 17.

---

* As in Prov. xx. 27 : " The *Ruach* (Heb. for *pneuma*) of man is the candle (or lamp) of Jehovah, searching all the inward parts of the belly."

† The A.V. of 1611 had " S," but current editions, with R.V., have " s."

John 16:13 "When he, the *pneuma* of truth, is come, (*i.e.*, shall have come) he will guide you into all truth." The A.V. of 1611 had " s "; but the current editions, with R.V., now have "S." Here, it is the great Giver and revealer of the truth of God Who is meant. He has guided into all truth (which could not then be revealed by the Lord Jesus: see verse 12). This promise of the Lord is very solemnly emphasised. *Eleven* times in these three verses (13, 14, 15), He says " shall" and " will."*

He must have fulfilled this promise, so surely made and so strongly confirmed. But, how has it been fulfilled? Surely not to each believer individually: otherwise, He gives one "truth" to one believer, and the opposite to another believer; so that they henceforth live in enmity, only to have a bitter controversy as to which one of them has "the truth." Surely not to believers collectively, so that one part of the "church" tortures and burns another part. "God is not the author of confusion"; still less of "envy, hatred and malice, and all uncharitableness."

How then has this sure promise been performed?

We submit that in "the Scriptures of truth," and especially in those Scriptures subsequently written in the Epistles addressed to the churches, the Spirit has guided the whole "Church of God" into "all truth."

In the Epistles addressed through Paul to the seven Churches (Romans, Corinthians, Galatians, Ephesians, Philippians, Colossians, and Thessalonians), He has revealed "all truth" necessary for, and relating to, the Church of God: making known the perfect standing of the believer "in Christ"; taking of the things of Christ, and showing them unto us, thus fulfilling the exact

* When He "is come" is literally *shall have* come (as in 2 Thess. i. 10, etc.)

promise of John xvi. 12-14, telling us what God has made Christ to be to us, and what He has made us to be " in Him." These are indeed " the things concerning Christ " which could not be revealed while he was on earth, nor until the Holy Spirit of Truth had come.

John 19:30 " He gave up the *pneuma*."* The usage here is *psychological*, according to Gen. ii. 7. Ecc. xii. 7. Ps. cxxxi. 5. Acts vii. 59.

John 20:22 " And when he had said this, he breathed on them, and said unto them, Receive ye *pneuma hagion*." †

What *pneuma hagion* means is clear from Luke xxiv. 49 (as we have shown above). There we are told that " the promise of the Father " was " power from on high." In Acts i. 4, 5, this " power from on high " is called "*pneuma hagion*." This they were baptized with (as the spiritual medium, in contrast with water, the material medium); and this they " received," as recorded in Acts ii. 4.

It is a great pity that this translation of *pneuma hagion* has led to a misuse of the words in the Church of England " ordering of Priests " (and of Bishops). There, when the Bishop lays his hands on their heads he says, " Receive the Holy Ghost for the Office and Work of a Priest in the Church of God, now committed unto thee by the imposition of our hands. Whose sins thou dost forgive, they are forgiven; and whose sins thou dost retain, they are retained," etc.

---

* The A.V. has " the ghost," and R.V. has " his spirit."

† Here there are no articles in the Greek; yet both the A.V. and R.V. translate it " the Holy Ghost," inserting the article, and using capital letters. In the margin the R.V. says, " or, *Holy Spirit*." But why put capital letters, when *pneuma hagion* always signifies the *gift* and not the Giver ?

Mortal men thus take the words of Christ into their own lips, and put ordinary mortals into the place of the Apostles. And this without the slightest warrant; and in spite of the fact that there is not a syllable to show that the Apostles themselves ever did, or ever had the authority to, pronounce those words, and give that gift to others: still less, that those others had the power to pass the gift on to others.

Whatever the words of the last clause (*v*. 23) mean, they relate only to those to whom they were then spoken. It is, therefore, quite unnecessary for us to discuss their meaning.

If the popular use of this passage be correct, some words are wanting to give it the needed support. Surely, the Lord would have said "And, when *you* pronounce these words over *others*, the same results will follow." But there is not a word of this. There is *a missing link*. And yet it is on this missing link that the whole fabric of Priestcraft is built up!

Something might be said if we saw any evidence of the actual conveyance of "spiritual gifts." But in the absence of these, it is making a very large demand on our credulity to ask us to admit such a claim: and it may well be called "the IMPOSITION of hands."

ACTS

Acts 1:2 "He was taken up, after that he through *pneuma hagion* had given commandments unto the apostles whom he had chosen." There are no articles here.* It is simply *pneuma hagion;* and it denotes the Divine power and authority with which He gave His commandments. All that He did was by this *Divine power*.

---

*Though the A.V. and R.V. insert it on their own responsibility, and use capital letters. The R.V. margin says "Or, *Holy Spirit:* and so throughout this book"; thus, not adding the article, but still using capital letters.

Acts 1:4,5 He "commanded them that they should not depart from Jerusalem, but wait for the promise of the Father which, saith he, ye have heard of me. For John, truly, baptized with water; but ye shall be baptized with *pneuma hagion* not many days hence."

It was the promise made by the Father; and we must here anticipate its fulfilment in chap. ii. 4 by remarking that the promise had to do with the kingdom, not with the church. It was made in Isa. xliv. 3.

"I will pour water upon him that is thirsty,
And floods upon the dry ground :
I will pour my spirit upon thy seed,
And my blessing upon thy offspring."

The same promise is referred to in Joel ii. 28, where the subject is the restoration of Israel; and the promise relates to the day when

"Jehovah will be jealous for his Land,
And pity his People " (*v.* 18).

After enumerating some of these outward and temporal blessings which will be the outcome of Jehovah's presence " in the midst of Israel," the prophet speaks of Divine and spiritual blessings with which God will bless His People, Israel.

"And it shall come to pass afterward (*i.e.*, after He has bestowed all these blessings on the Land), that

" I will pour out my spirit upon all flesh ;
And your sons and your daughters shall prophesy,
Your old men shall dream dreams,
Your young men shall see visions :
And also upon the servants and upon the handmaids in those days
Will I pour out my spirit.
And I will show wonders in the heavens
And in the earth,
Blood, and fire, and pillars of smoke.

The sun shall be turned into darkness,
And the moon into blood,
Before the great and the terrible DAY OF THE
    LORD come.
And it shall come to pass,
That whosoever shall call on the name of the
    LORD shall be delivered:
For in MOUNT ZION and in JERUSALEM
    shall be deliverance,
As the LORD hath said, and in the remnant whom
    the LORD shall call,
For, behold, IN THOSE DAYS, AND IN THAT
    TIME,
When I shall bring again the captivity of JUDAH
    and JERUSALEM,
I will also gather," etc. (Joel ii. 28—iii. 2).

Surely it is marvellous that any who really study " the
Word of Truth" could have so wrongly divided it as to
interpret this of the Church of God.

In Acts i. and ii. there was a re-proclamation of the kingdom. The keys had been given to Peter ;—the " keys
of the kingdom " mark, and not the keys of the church :
(for the Pope's pretensions are based on the same
wrong dividing, and therefore wrong interpretations, of
" the Word of Truth").

It was a last proclamation of blessing for Israel on
the one and only condition of *national repentance.* " Repent " was this one condition. " Repent," and ye shall receive the gift of *the pneuma hagion :* for the promise is unto
you and to your children (Isa. xliv. 3 ; Acts ii. 38, 39).

This promise of Joel ii., and this call of Peter, have
nothing to do with the church, or with this present Dis.
pensation, or with " Infant Baptism." They have to do
with *the national repentance of the People of Israel.*

" Repent," he says, and this promise shall be fulfilled in you, now.

Again he makes the proclamation, and again he uses the key of Israel* in Acts iii. 19-26 (R.V.). Peter says:

" Repent ye therefore, and turn again, that your sins may be blotted out, that so there may come seasons of refreshing from the presence of the Lord ; and that he may send the Christ (*i.e.*, the Messiah) who hath been appointed for you, even Jesus : whom the heaven must receive until the times of restoration of all things, whereof God spake by the mouth of his holy prophets which have been since the world began. Moses indeed said, A prophet shall the Lord God raise up unto you from among your brethren, like unto me (marg., Or, *as* he raised up *me*) ; to him shall ye hearken in all things whatsoever he shall speak unto you. And it shall be, that every soul, which shall not hearken to that prophet, shall be utterly destroyed from among the people. Yea and all the prophets from Samuel and them that followed after, as many as have spoken, they also told of these days. Ye are the sons of the prophets, and of the covenant which God made (marg. Gr. *covenanted*) with your fathers, saying unto Abraham, And in thy seed shall all the families of the earth be blessed. Unto you first God, having raised up his Servant, sent him to bless you, in turning away every one of you from your iniquities " (Acts iii. 19-26 R.V.).

It seems impossible for us to interpret these words of the Church of God—the Body of Christ, seeing that the Mystery or Secret of the Church had not yet been revealed: inasmuch as the Church was never the subject of Old Testament prophecy; but that Mystery was " kept secret since the world began " (Rom. xvi. 25) : and " from the beginning of the world hath been hid in

---

* As in Acts x., xi., he uses the other key, for Gentile blessing.

God" (Eph. iii. 9): "even the Secret which hath been hid from ages and generations" (Col. i. 26).

Peter was using "the keys of the kingdom," which had been committed to him; and was proclaiming, and opening the doors of, the kingdom. But the People, through their Rulers, again rejected the Messiah. Christ had gone "to receive for Himself a Kingdom and to return"; but they sent a messenger after him, saying, "we will not have this man to reign over us." Here was the fulfilment of the Lord's parable of Luke xix. 12-14.

"His citizens hated him"; and, instead of repenting, they imprisoned those who proclaimed Him. They stoned Stephen; they slew James with the sword; and would have slain Peter also, but for his miraculous deliverance.

So, the kingdom and all its blessings, with the fulfilment of Joel ii., are now all in abeyance; while the Church, the Body of Christ, is being taken out.

The stoning of Stephen (Acts vii.) was shortly followed by the call of Paul (Acts ix.); and, indeed, was over-ruled to bring it about.

The killing of James and the imprisonment of Peter (Acts xii.) were followed by the commissioning of Paul, and the sending him forth on his wondrous ministry. (Acts xiii. 1-3).

The exhaustive fulfilment of the promise of Joel is still in abeyance: and it will not now be fulfilled until "the great and terrible day of the Lord come." When the judgments of Rev. viii., ix., and Matt. xxiv. 29-31, shall have been poured out, then, "afterward," shall *pneuma hagion* be poured forth "upon all flesh."

Pneuma hagion was the promise of the Father (Luke xxiv. 49; John xiv. 16, 26, 27; xv. 26; xvi. 7;

Acts ii. 33). It was the *spiritual* medium with which they were to be baptized instead of *material* water.

The promise of Acts i. 5, was performed in Acts ii. 4. It was strictly in connection with the kingdom, and with Israel; and had nothing to do with the Church, or the Gentiles.*

The expression *pneuma hagion*, therefore, in Acts i. 5, relates to *the gift*, and not to the Giver. For, the moment it was given, the effect was seen :—" they were all filled with *pneuma hagion*, and began to speak with other tongues, as the Spirit gave them utterance " (see below under Acts ii. 4).

Acts 1:8 The Lord here, again, identifies *pneuma hagion* with " power from on high," as being the *gift* of the Holy Spirit.

" Ye shall receive power after that *the hagion pneuma* is come upon you; and ye shall be witnesses unto me."

None can be witnesses for Him before they are endowed with this " power," which, as *pneuma hagion*, is the *gift* of the Holy Spirit, the Giver.

The article is used here, grammatically, merely to refer it back to, and identify it with verse 5. But the A.V. and R.V. again wrongly use capital letters.

---

* " This is that " (Acts ii. 16). What is the " this "? and what is the " that "? To what do these pronouns refer? Peter's words commence with " But," introducing a new argument in rebutting the charge of drunkenness. The pronoun "this" is emphatic: and refers not to the event, or to the speaking, but to the prophecy of Joel in the words which follow (*vv.* 17-21). The argument was that the speaking with tongues need not proceed from wine, inasmuch as similar speaking was prophesied of "the last days." *That* speaking would be the result of the pouring out of Divine *pneuma*. Why then should not this be produced by the same cause. Peter does not say, " This event is *the fulfilment* of Joel": but, " This (which follows) is what Joel says of a future similar event."

Acts 1:16 " This scripture must needs have been fulfilled which *the pneuma, the holy*, by the mouth of David, spake before concerning Judas."

Here, it is the Holy Spirit, the Giver and Inspirer of that scripture, by David. The definite article is used with each of the two words, and we have the full expression, to show us that it was the Holy Spirit Himself in operation.

It was David's mouth that spake, but they were not David's words.

Here we have the clearest definition of what Inspiration is : and no one can explain the mystery to us beyond this.

Acts 2:4 (twice). " They were all filled with *pneuma hagion.*" Here it is not the Giver, but it is the gift; and the gift is " the gift of tongues " (1 Cor. xii. 10, 11) ; for it is immediately added, that they " began to SPEAK with other tongues as *the pneuma* gave them utterance." Here, it is the Giver, giving them utterance.

The fact that *pneuma* is used twice in this verse is of great service to us : because the article with the second occurrence distinguishes the Giver from His gift; and the Divine worker from His operations. It shows that in the former we have the *gift*, and in the latter we have the Giver.*

This fulfilment of the promise should be studied in connection with what has been said about the promise under ch. i. 5.

Acts 2:17 " I will pour out of my *pneuma* (Lit., of *the pneuma* [of me]) upon all flesh."

---

*Strange to say, the A.V. of 1611 has " the holy Ghost " in the first clause, and " the spirit " in the second. Current editions, however, with the R.V., have capital letters in both clauses.

Acts 2:18 "And on my servants and on my hand-maidens I will pour out in those days of my *pneuma* (Lit., of *the pneuma* [of me]); and they shall prophesy."

Here, in both these verses, we have the pouring out; a term inapplicable to a Person, but most appropriate of gifts. A person can pour out, but how can he be poured out? Moreover, we are distinctly told what it was that was to be poured out; *viz.*, " *the gift of prophesying.*"

Acts 2:33 "Having received from the Father the promise of *the hagion pneuma* he hath shed forth (or poured out) this, which ye now see and hear."

Here, all the Critical Texts and R.V. read "*the pneuma the holy.*" But, even if they be correct, the articles are used only grammatically, to identify it with the *pneuma hagion* of verse 4, which is the subject of the whole chapter.

It cannot be the Holy Spirit; for He is *pneuma*; He cannot be seen except by the effects (See John iii. 8 above). Whatever "this" was that was poured out, it could be both *seen* and *heard* (ch. ii. 33). It must therefore refer to the gifts, which were both visible and audible, and not to the Giver.

Acts 2:38 "Ye shall receive the gift of *the hagion pneuma.*" Here the "gift" is so called, and is clearly distinguished from the Giver, who is the Holy Spirit.

Acts 4:8 "Then Peter filled with *pneuma hagion*": *i.e.*, with "power from on high," or Divine power manifested in the gift of speaking according to the promise of Matt. x. 20. (Compare 2 Sam. xxiii. 2. 2 Tim. iv. 17.)

It was *the gift* of speaking; and this was given by the

great Giver of all spiritual power. Acts vi. 10 throws further light on this. (See below.)

Both A.V. and R.V. again insert the English definite article, though there is none in the Greek.

Acts 4:25   This is the first of the three passages* which have to be added, where *pneuma* is not found in the Textus Receptus.

The A V. reads "Who by the mouth of thy servant David hast said." But all the Critical Greek Texts and the R.V. read "who by *pneuma hagion*, by the mouth of our father David thy servant, didst say" (referring to Psalm ii.).

Whether these be correct or not, it was by "power from on high," *i.e.*, by Divine inspiration that David spoke and wrote that Psalm.

Acts 4:31   "They were all filled with *pneuma hagion*."

All the Critical Greek Texts read "*the hagion pneuma*": but either reading shows that *spiritual gifts* are meant; for the speaking the Word of God with boldness is mentioned as the gift that was here specially given. Both A.V. and R.V. add the articles and use capital letters.

Acts 5:3   "Why hath Satan filled thine heart [for] thee to lie † to *the pneuma the holy ?*" *i.e.*, to the Holy Spirit.

Acts 5:9   "How is it that ye have agreed together

---

* The other two are Phil. iv. 23 and Rev. xxii. 6.

† This verb ψεύδεσθαι *(pseudesthai)*, in its twelve occurrences in the New Testament, is used absolutely in (at least) eight, once with εἰς *(eis) to*, following (Col. iii. 9) ; once with κατά *(kata) against,* (Jas. iii. 14). In Acts v. 3 we have it used first with an *Acc.*, and, in verse 4, with a *Dative.* So we might preserve this distinction by rendering the two passages thus : "to overreach the Holy Spirit" *(v.* 3) ; and "thou hast not lied to men, but to God."

to tempt *the pneuma* of the Lord?" The article points back to verse 3, and shows it is the Holy Spirit who is here meant.

Acts 5:16 "Them which were vexed with unclean *pneumata*": *i.e.,* with demons.

Acts 5:32 "And we are * witnesses of these things; and [so is] *the pneuma the holy*, also, which God gave to them that obey Him."

Here, though there are two articles, they are used grammatically: for the Aorist verb points back to the definite gift which the Holy Spirit "gave" in Acts ii. 4. That gift is there said to be "*pneuma hagion.*" And the articles here (as in chap. xi. 16) are used to identify this gift with that giving.

Acts 6:3 "Look ye out seven men...full of *pneuma hagion*† and wisdom, whom we may appoint over this business."

If the A.V. and R.V. correctly interpret this of "the Holy Spirit," then it is possible to be full of "the Holy Spirit" and yet be destitute of "wisdom." Can this be correct? Can it be possible? Does not this stamp as false and untenable the whole system of translating *pneuma hagion* as though it were the Giver instead of His Gifts?

Here, the matter in question is specially declared to be "business"; and for this, something more was required than *spirituality*. A man might be very spiritual but most unbusinesslike. He might be able to pray, or speak, but be a baby in matters of business. He might be good in teaching, but bad at accounts. So, what was required was seven men, who were filled with spiritual gifts, *plus*

---

* Tisch. and Tregelles and R.V. omit "his."

† All the Critical Texts and R.V. omit the word *hagion* (holy). But both the A.V. and R.V. insert the article and use capital letters.

" wisdom," which was the special gift necessary to deal with business matters.

The gifts of " tongues " or " healing," etc., would not be sufficient where the gift of " wisdom " was specially called for and needed.

This proves that *pneuma hagion*, by itself, must not be interpreted of the Giver, but of His Gifts.

Acts 6:5 " And they chose Stephen, a man full of faith, and of *pneuma hagion*."*

The use of *pneuma* in this chapter, and its interchange and combination with various spiritual gifts, is most instructive, and valuable, because it throws a flood of light on the whole subject.

We learn what this *pneuma hagion* was, of which Stephen was " full." It consisted of " wisdom " (*v.* 3), " faith " (*v.* 5), " faith and power," " wonders and miracles "† (*v.* 8), and also in verse 10 " the wisdom and *pneuma* by which he spake " and which his enemies could not " withstand."‡

From this we learn that Stephen's speaking was by direct Inspiration ; for *pneuma hagion* denotes the spiritual power which was the Gift of the Great Giver (the Holy Spirit) to him.§

This should forever stop our mouths in speaking of " discrepancies " which the natural man thinks he sees in Stephen's address in Acts vii.

---

* The A.V. of 1611 used a small " h " and put " the holy Ghost." Current editions put " H." The R.V. translates " the Holy Spirit."

† Greek " *wonders and signs*." See R.V.

‡ The word rendered " resist " here (in A.V.) is ἀνθίστημι *(anthistēmi) to withstand*. This his enemies could not do. The word rendered " resist " in ch. vii. 51 is ἀντιπίπτω *(antipiptō) to fall against :* this His enemies could do, and did.

§ The A.V. of 1611 and current editions have " s " here, as in *v.* 10. But R.V. has " S." Both Versions insert the article.

When man finds a "difficulty" it never seems to dawn on him that the difficulty is in his own head! He always thinks there is something corrupt in the text, or wrong with the translation; but he never seems to suspect that what is wrong is, in all probability, in himself.

Stephen's inspired address is perfect in Divine wisdom and truth. His enemies, at any rate, were "not able to withstand" it; but the critics to-day do withstand it; though they only fall against it to their own confusion.

Acts 7:51   "Ye do always resist* *the pneuma, the holy*."

Here it is the Holy Spirit, who has spoken by His prophets. The People ever opposed themselves to His testimony, and slew His prophets with the sword. Stephen goes on at once to show that he referred to the Holy Spirit's testimony by His prophets; for he asks:—"Which of the prophets have not your fathers persecuted?"

They could not "withstand" the Holy Spirit's words in His prophets; but they could, and did, "resist" those words, by putting the prophets to death.

Acts 7:55   "But he, being full of *pneuma hagion* (*i.e.*, of Divine power and grace), looked up steadfastly into heaven." There is no article; and it is not the Giver, but His Divine gift of grace, and His sustaining power.

Acts 7:59   "And they stoned Stephen, calling upon [God] and saying, Lord Jesus receive my *pneuma*." His Lord had himself thus called on the Father, Luke xxiii. 46, according to Ps. xxxi. 5, and Ecc. xii. 7. The

---

* See note on ch. vi. 5, page 93.

word *pneuma*, here, is used psychologically.   Both A.V. and R.V. have "s."

Acts 8:7   "For unclean *pneumata*, crying with a loud voice, came out of them": *i.e.*, demons, as in ch. v. 16.

Acts 8:15   " Who when they were come down, prayed for them, that they might receive *pneuma hagion* " : *i.e.*, spiritual gifts, according to Luke xi. 13.

Both A.V. and R.V. add the article and use capital letters.

Acts 8:17   " They laid their hands on them, and they received *pneuma hagion*."

As John xx. 22 has been misused in connection with the " Ordering of Priests " in the Church of England, ever since the Reformation ; so Acts viii. has been perverted in like manner in connection with "Confirmation," but only in very recent times.

"The Order of Confirmation" according to the Prayer-Book of the Church of England, says nothing whatever about the *giving* or *receiving* the Holy Spirit. On the contrary, the prayer for those on whom the Bishop lays his hands, is : " daily increase in them Thy manifold GIFTS of grace; the spirit of wisdom and understanding; the spirit of counsel and ghostly strength; the spirit of knowledge and true godliness; and fill them O Lord, with the spirit of Thy holy fear, now and for ever.   Amen."

And all this with a small " s."

It is quite a sign of the times that there has been, only of late years, an attempt on the part of certain Bishops to make an unfair and unwarrantable use of this mistranslation of Acts viii. 17 ; forcing it, and using it for a departure not only from Bible doctrine, but from Prayer-Book teaching, and the Reformation settlement.

The Bishop of London, in his "Pastoral "* (1904), boldly overrides the simple Prayer-Book service by saying, " It needed the long preparation of the world before the Incarnation, the Incarnation itself, the Agony and Bloody Sweat, the Death upon the Cross, the Resurrection, and finally the Ascension, before a ' Confirmation ' became possible."

What does this mean if it does not recognise "Confirmation " as a Romish Sacrament.†

Bishop Gore, of Worcester, (1904), actually goes so far as to add to the Prayer-Book service by requesting the candidates to repeat the words, " I am here to receive the gift of the Holy Ghost by the laying on of the Bishop's hands."‡

We affirm that this addition is not only illegal as an act; but it is Anti-Reformation and Romish in character. It is a new departure altogether.

Archbishop Cranmer, referring to this passage in connection with this subject, says,§ "these acts were done by a special gift given to the apostles for the confirmation of God's Word, at that time "; and that "the said special gift does not now remain with the successors of the Apostles." That " the bishop, in the name of the Church, doth invoke the Holy Spirit to give strength and constancy with other spiritual gifts, unto the person confirmed."

Bishop Jewell says‖ of this act of the apostles. " It is not so now . . . there is no such miracle wrought.

---

* It is not our province here to question his right to order this to be read by Evangelical Clergymen, though it is a right only by courtesy.

† See *The Protestant Churchman*, Jan., 1904.

‡ Which was done on March 4, 1904, according to *The News* (Upton-on-Severn).

§ *Cranmer's Remains and Letters*, Parker Society, page 80.

‖ Bishop Jewell. *Treatise on the Sacraments.* Works. Part II. Parker Society, page 1126.

There is no need that it should so be. There was no commandment either to appoint it to the church, or to continue it until the coming of Christ."

The doctrine of the Anti-Reformation Bishops, to-day, is not the doctrine of the Church to which they profess to belong.

No wonder the Prayer-Book suffers, when the Bible itself is set at nought.

Church Officers, and Professors, to-day, use the power and influence conferred on them, for undoing the work for which they were set apart.

They were all of them asked at their ordination, " Do you unfeignedly believe all the Canonical Scriptures of the Old and New Testament ? " and they all of them answered, " *I do believe them.*"

They were all of them asked, " Will you be ready, with all faithful diligence, to banish and drive away all erroneous and strange doctrines contrary to God's Word . . . ? " and they all of them answered, " *I will, the Lord being my helper.*"

In spite of these promises many are using the influence derived from their dignities and their emoluments to undermine the Word of God, and to bring in novel and strange doctrines, not only contrary to the Scripture, but opposed to the Prayer-Book.

In the commercial world, a man who received his pay from one firm and did the work of another would be dismissed at a moment's notice. In the Naval or Military Service, he would be drummed out in time of peace, and in time of war he would be shot. It is only in the " Church " and in " Religion " that such an outrage is not only tolerated and condoned, but is a stepping-stone to promotion, and this, to the undoing of the " Church " and the inconceivable injury to the first principles of morality: the effect of which must be felt in the lowering of morals throughout the country.

It is a pity that the mistranslation of *pneuma hagion* in Acts viii. 17 should afford any ground for such dishonesty.

Acts 8:18 " When Simon saw that through laying on of the apostles' hands *the pneuma, the holy* was given."

Here the words " the holy," are omitted by all the critical Greek Texts and R.V., and are put within brackets, as doubtful, by Tregelles. But in either case the article or articles refer back to the *pneuma hagion* spoken of in verses 15, 17.

Acts 8:19 " Give me also this power, that on whomsoever I lay hands, he may receive *pneuma hagion*." There is no article here; and, as in all other similar passages where these words are so used, they denote the gift and not the giver : *i.e.*, the gift mentioned in *vv.* 15, 17. Both A.V. and R.V. add the article and use capitals.

Acts 8:29 " Then *the pneuma* said to Philip." The article refers us back to " the angel of the Lord " mentioned in verse 26, for angels are made and called *pneumata* or *spirits* (Ps. civ. 4, Heb. i. 7), because they " have not flesh and bones," as a risen and " changed " human body has (See Luke xxiv. 39), nor have they " flesh and blood " as a mortal human body has. Both A.V. and R.V. wrongly use a " S " as in verse 39.

Acts 8:39 " A *pneuma* of the Lord (*pneuma Kyriou*) caught away Philip ": *i.e.*, the angel already mentioned in verses 26 and 29. Compare chap. x. 19 and xi. 12 below for a similar usage of *pneuma*.

Acts 9:17 " The Lord, even Jesus ... hath sent

me (Ananias) that thou (Saul) mightest receive thy sight, and be filled with *pneuma hagion* ": *i.e.*, with "power from on high," as the Eleven had been filled in John xx. 22, and the Twelve in Acts ii. Both A.V. and R.V. add the article and use capitals.

Acts 9:31 " Then had the churches rest throughout all Judea ... and walking in the comfort of (*i.e.*, given by) *the hagion pneuma* were multiplied."

Here it is the Holy Spirit as the giver of the comfort, strengthening them and enabling them to walk in " the fear of the Lord."

Acts 10:19 " While Peter thought on the vision, *the pneuma* said to him ": *i.e.*, the spiritual being already spoken of in verse 3 as " an angel of God." The A.V. of 1611 had " s." But the current editions with R.V. have " S." Compare viii. 31, and xi. 12, for a similar usage of *pneuma.*

Acts 10:38 " How God anointed Jesus of Nazareth with *pneuma hagion* and power," as recorded in Luke iv. 1, etc. The A.V. and R.V. interpolate the article and use capitals.

Acts 10:44 " While Peter yet spake these words *the pneuma the holy* fell on all them which heard the word." Although there are two articles here, their use is only for grammatical emphasis, in order to identify what is said with ch. ii. 4. See verses 45 and 47 below.

Acts 10:45 " On the Gentiles also was poured out the gift of the *hagion pneuma.*" Here it is either the Gen. of Apposition, in which case *hagion pneuma* is the gift; or, it is the Gen. of Origin, in which case it is the Holy Spirit the Giver of the Gift.

Acts 10:47 " These . . . which have received *the pneuma the holy*, as we also [received it] ? "

They had received *pneuma hagion* in ch. ii. 4; and these Gentiles received nothing different from, and nothing more than the Twelve received then.

Acts 11:12   " *The pneuma* bade me go with them " : *i.e.*, the angel, or spiritual being, mentioned already in ch. x. 3, and 19.   The A.V. of 1611, and current editions have a small " s " here.   The R.V. has " S."   Compare ch. viii. 31, and x. 19, for a similar usage of *pneuma.*

Acts 11:15   " And as I began to speak, *the pneuma the holy* fell on them, as on us at the beginning."

Here, these concluding words clearly show that the definite articles are used to refer us back to that beginning described in ch. ii. 4.   For in the next verse that which fell on them is definitely spoken of as *pneuma hagion* ; and in verse 17, is spoken of as " the like gift," which, we know from ch. ii. 4, was " *pneuma hagion.*"

Acts 11:16   " Ye shall be baptised with *pneuma hagion* ": *i.e.*, with " power from on high."   See usage No. XIV., Acts i. 4, 5.   The A.V. and R.V. both insert the article and use capitals ; thus making no distinction between this and verse 15, where there are two articles in the Greek.

Acts 11:24   " He (Barnabas) was a good man and full of *pneuma hagion*": *i.e.*, full of Divine power, and spiritual gifts.   Both A.V. and R.V. insert the article and use capitals.

Acts 11:28   " Agabus . . . signified by *the pneuma.*"
Here it was the Holy Spirit revealing Himself through Agabus.   Though the Greek has the article, the A.V. has a small " s."   The R.V. has a capital " S."

Acts 13:2   " *The pneuma the holy* said, Separate

me Barnabas and Saul for the work whereunto I have called them."

Here it is God (the Holy Spirit Himself) in solemn action, commencing the special ministry and teaching of the Apostle Paul. Here, hands were laid upon him, solemnly setting him apart for this wondrous work. Here, his Hebrew name, Saul, was changed to the Gentile name, Paul. Here, also, is the dividing line between the two halves of the Acts of the Apostles.

The first half is occupied with Peter's ministry in the Land of Israel, ending with his imprisonment; and, after his deliverance, going to "another place," and disappearing from the page of history.

The last half of the Acts is occupied with Paul's ministry among the Gentiles, ending with his imprisonment likewise. He too, or rather his ministry, has disappeared from history. But with this difference that while there was "no small stir . . . what was become of Peter" (ch. xii. 18), there is, to-day, no stir at all as to what has become of Paul and his teaching!

That teaching was given up even in his own lifetime (see 2 Tim. i. 15, compared with Acts xix. 10). Paul has been deposed. Peter has been found: and he and his "keys" have been placed at the head of the professing Church! While the teaching of Paul has been replaced by "the Teaching of the Twelve."

Acts 13:4   "So they, being sent forth by *the pneuma the holy*, departed." Here all the Critical Texts and R.V. read "the holy pneuma." But, whichever is the true reading, it refers back, here, to verse 2, and denotes the Holy Spirit Himself.

Acts 13:9   "Then Saul (who also is called Paul) filled with *pneuma hagion*," (or, "power from high").

Both A.V. and R.V. insert the Eng. article and use capitals, as in *v.* 52.

Acts 13:52   "The disciples were filled with joy, and *pneuma hagion*" : *i.e.*, with spiritual gifts, of which "joy" was one (Gal. v. 22).

Acts 15:8   "God who knoweth the hearts bare them witness, giving them *the pneuma the holy*, even as he did unto us."

These last words, "as he did unto us," point back to ch. ii. 4 ; and show that the articles are used grammatically, in order to identify this gift of *pneuma hagion* to believing Gentiles in Acts x. 44 as being the same as that bestowed upon believing Jews in ch. ii. 4.

Acts 15:28   "It seemed good to *the holy pneuma*, and to us."   Here the context, together with the articles, clearly shows that the Holy Spirit is meant.

Acts 16:6   " They . . . were forbidden by *the hagion pneuma* to preach the Word in Asia."   The context and definite article show that the Holy Spirit is meant, although the expression is not the full one generally used when He is meant.

Acts 16:7   "*The pneuma** suffered them not" (to go into Bythinia).

Here, the Holy Spirit is meant, as in *v.* 6.

These two actions of the Holy Spirit clearly show that the expression, "all nations," in Matt. xxviii. 19, is not to be interpreted of this present dispensation of Grace, or understood in the popular missionary sense : but that God's openings and closings, and leadings and guidings, are to be looked for and obeyed.   Missionary work, as well as our own private affairs, is all subject to

---

* All the Critical Texts and R.V. add " of Jesus ": *i.e.* : the Spirit sent and promised by Jesus.

His will. "Even so, Father; for so it seemed good in Thy sight," is to be our attitude (Matt. xi. 26) in the presence of the "closed door," as well as in the light of what we call "failure." "All that the Father giveth me shall come to me" (John vi. 37). There can, therefore, be no failure (except in our faithfulness), and should be no disappointment as to the Lord's real work.

Acts 16:16   "*A pneuma* of Python": *i.e.*, an evil spirit of some special kind: a Python-spirit.

Acts 16:18   "Paul said to *the pneuma*." The article points back to the evil spirit mentioned in verse 16. It thus illustrates the grammatical use referred to in similar cases; and shows that "the spirit" does not necessarily mean the Holy Spirit.

Acts 17:16   "Paul's......*pneuma* was stirred within him."

Here *pneuma* is put by *Metonymy* (of the Cause) for his feelings, which were painfully excited within him. Both A.V. and R.V. have a small "s" here.

Acts 18:5   This is the third passage in which the word "*pneuma*" is omitted by all the Critical Greek Texts, and the R.V. They all read συνείχετο τῳ λόγῳ (*suneicheto tō logō*) *engrossed with the word* (instead of συνείχετο τῷ πνεύματι (*suneichetō tō pneumati*) *pressed in spirit*): or, perhaps, better still, *engrossed with his discourse: i.e.*, his testimony; which is in harmony with the context, for it goes on to tell us how he "testified to the Jews that Jesus was the Messiah."

Acts 18:25   "Apollos was fervent as to *the pneuma* [of him]": *i.e.*, fervent in his *pneuma: i.e.*, according to the Hebrew *Idiom*, very zealous and diligent in spiritual things (Compare Rom. xii. 11, and see usage No. X.). Both A.V. and R.V. have a small "s."

Acts 19:2   (twice) "Did ye receive *pneuma hagion**
when† ye believed ?" *i.e.,* Did ye receive spiritual
gifts when ye believed.   Paul's teaching was that
no one could believe without the Holy Spirit's enabling power.   He could not, therefore, have meant
to ask whether they had, by believing, merited or become
entitled to the work of the Holy Spirit ; but, had they
received any of the spiritual gifts which He then or
afterwards bestows, " as He will," upon believers.

They replied that they had not heard anything about
spiritual gifts (*pneuma hagion*).

They must have known about the Holy Spirit: but
Ephesus was a long way from Jerusalem, and Samaria,
and Cæsarea, where the spiritual gifts had been previously given ; so that they had not heard anything about
them ; just as those in Cæsarea had not heard of the
spiritual gifts in Jerusalem (Acts x.).   "And he (Paul)
said, Into (we quote from the R.V.) what then were ye
baptized ? And they said, Into John's baptism.

Acts 19:4   " And Paul said,
> John baptized with the baptism of repentance,
> saying unto the people, that they should believe
> on him which should come after him, that is,
> on Jesus.‡ (5) And when they heard this, they
> were baptized into the name of the Lord
> Jesus."

---

* Both A.V. and R.V. insert the article without any warrant,
and create a difficulty by using *capitals*. They therefore make
no difference between verse 2 and verse 6, where there are two
articles.

† There is nothing in the Greek about "since" or "after." It
is simply the participle *having believed*, or, on believing : or, with
R.V., *when ye believed*.

‡ All the Critical Greek Texts, with R.V. omit " Christ."

Acts 19:6 "And when Paul had laid his hands on them, *the pneuma the hagion*, came on them ; and they spake with tongues, and prophesied." The articles refer us back to verse 2. The fifth verse is usually taken as the resumption of the narrative of Luke ; as though Luke went on to give an account of what Paul *did* after what he had *said* in verse 4. But we believe that in verse 5 we have the *continuation* of the words of Paul, and of what Paul was saying. Paul (in *vv.* 4, 5) is telling these Ephesian believers what John said and did. It is not Luke, breaking off suddenly, and telling us, in verse 5, what Paul did.

It is important for us to define who are the "they" of verse 5.

Who were "they" ? Were they those who heard John, or those who were listening to Paul? We believe they were those who heard John, and not those who heard Paul: otherwise we have here the only case of re-baptism mentioned in the New Testament : which, to say the least, is rather startling.

Paul finds no fault with John's baptism ; for it was "from heaven." But he says that they were baptized unto repentance and in the faith of *a coming Messiah ;* and goes on to speak of the faith of those who heard John as evidenced by their being baptized into the name of Him who John said should come after him; *i.e.,* in the name of the Lord Jesus.

It is not till verse 6 that Luke again takes up and goes on with his account of what Paul *did*, after he has told us of what Paul had *said*, in verses 4 and 5.

(6) "And when Paul had laid his hands upon them, *the pneuma the holy* came upon them, and they spake with tongues and prophesied." These were the spiritual gifts which they received with the laying on of Paul's hands. The articles are used grammatically to refer us

back to the *pneuma hagion* of verse 2. It does not say that Paul re-baptized them. The contrast is *not* between John's baptism with water, and Paul's re-baptism with water; but between John's baptism with water (*vv.* 4, 5), and Paul's baptism with *pneuma hagion* (*v.* 6).

"Laying on of hands" was one of the "first principles" of the "doctrine of Christ" (Heb. vi. 1-4. Compare 1 Tim. iv. 14, 2 Tim. i. 6). It was a solemn act of public and authoritative sanction and designation. Paul exercised it here in the bestowal of spiritual gifts, after he had told them what John said and did, and had thus shown the difference between John's baptism with water, and the new baptism with *pneuma hagion*, instituted by Christ.

The interpretation given above is borne out by

THE STRUCTURE OF ACTS xix. 1-8

A | 1.   Paul's arrival at Ephesus.

   B | 1.   Certain men there.   Their character: "Disciples."

      C | 2.   Spiritual gifts: their ignorance of them.

         D | 3.   What they had received: "John's baptism."

            E | 4, 5.   What Paul said.   (Paul's description of John's action).

            E | 6-.   What Paul did.   (Luke's description of Paul's action).

         D | 6-.   What they now received: Spiritual gifts: (*pneuma hagion*).

      C | -6.   Spiritual gifts: their use of them.

   B | 7.   The men.   Their number: "about twelve."

A | 8.   Paul's continuance at Ephesus.

In this Structure we have all the members exquisitely balanced: and the Correspondence is perfect and complete.

We have John's baptism standing out (in D) in contrast with *pneuma hagion* (in *D*), which was to supersede it as stated again and again. See Matt. iii. 11. Acts i. 5; xi. 16.

The material element of water was to give place to the spiritual element of Divine power and gifts.

What we have in Acts xix. therefore, is no case of re-baptism with water by Paul: but an object-lesson illustrating the important fact which lies at the threshold of the Acts of the Apostles, furnishing the key to the understanding of that book ; and of the essential character of the new Dispensation of Grace, which distinguishes it from the old Dispensation of Works.

Acts 19:12   " The evil *pneumata* went out of them " (plural).

Acts 19:13   The same as verse 12.

Acts 19:15   " The evil *pneuma* answered and said, Jesus I know, and Paul I understand very well ; but who are ye ? "

Acts 19:16   " The man in whom the evil *pneuma* was leaped on them."

Acts 19:21   " Paul purposed in his *pneuma*." This is an Idiomatic Hebrew usage of the word *pneuma*, meaning that Paul was firmly resolved. (See usage No. X). Both A.V. and R.V. have a small " s."

Acts 20:22   " And now behold I go bound as to (my) *pneuma* ": *lit.* " as to *the pneuma* [of me]" : *i.e., firmly resolved*, as in ch. xix. 21. Both A.V. and R.V. have a small " s." (See usage No. X).

Acts 20:23   "*The pneuma the holy* witnesseth in every city saying that bonds and afflictions abide me."

This is the Holy Spirit in action, speaking through His servants the prophets. (See usage No. X).

Acts 20:28   "The flock over which *the pneuma the holy* hath made you overseers."   Here, the articles and the context fix the meaning as denoting the Holy Spirit.

Acts 21:4   Certain " disciples . . . said to Paul by *the pneuma* " : *i.e.*, by the Holy Spirit as the source of all prophecy: the article referring back to ch. xx. 23.

Acts 23:8   " The Sadducees say that there is . . . neither angel, nor *pneuma* " : (*i.e.*, neither angel nor any spiritual being).   The A.V. and R.V. both have " s," and " A."

Acts 23:9   " If a *pneuma* or an angel hath spoken to him, let us not fight against God."   The same as in verse 8.   The A.V. and R.V. both have " s " and " a." But the A.V. 1611 had " s " and " A."

Acts 28:25   " Well spake *the pneuma the holy* by Isaiah the prophet." Here, it is the Holy Spirit Himself speaking by Isaiah : showing us that, in Isaiah vi., we have Isaiah's voice and Isaiah's pen, but not Isaiah's words.   Compare Acts i. 16.

ROMANS

Rom. 1:4   In this passage the nature of the Lord Jesus
is being set forth. God's gospel is " concerning His Son
Jesus Christ ": hence, it is necessary, at the outset,
to define His true nature.   As regards his *flesh* He was
" of the Seed of David."   As regards his *pneuma* He was
"the Son of God." And this *pneuma* was "holiness" itself.
The word is remarkable : it is ἁγιωσύνη (*hagiōsunē*).   It
does not occur at all in Greek Literature.   And in the
New Testament it is found only here, and 2 Cor. vii. 1
(" perfecting *holiness* in the fear of God "), and 1 Thess.
iii. 13 (" unblameable in *holiness* before God ").   The
expression " *pneuma hagiōsunēs* " must therefore not
be confounded with *pneuma hagion*.   *Hagiōsunē* denotes
the attribute of *holiness* itself ; not merely holy as to
character.   Hence, " *pneuma hagiōsunēs*," *a pneuma of
holiness*, being the Genitive of Apposition, means a
pneuma which is holiness itself.   This agrees with Luke
i. 35 where it is distinctly stated to Mary : " that holy
thing which shall be born of thee shall be called the
Son of God."   The Divine spiritual nature of Christ
which He had from the Holy Spirit Himself is here put
in contrast with the human flesh which he had of
" Mary " as " the Seed of David."

Accordingly, at His birth He was declared to be
"the Son of God."   And being the Son of God, " it was
not possible that he should be holden of death ";
therefore " God raised Him from the dead " (Acts
ii. 24) ; and by His resurrection He was thus by Divine
power declared to be the Son of God."*

---

* We have elsewhere translated this "by a resurrection of
dead persons," quoting Matt. xxvii. 52-54.   But the context in
Rom. i. 4 seems to require Christ's own resurrection ; though
the other may be included, on account of the greatness of the
" power " put forth.

"As to flesh" He was put to death. "As to *pneuma*" He was raised from the dead. This is also the argument in 1 Pet. iii. 18, where there is neither article nor preposition. (See below.) In Rom. i. 4, the A.V. of 1611 had "S"; but, strange to say, the current editions now print it with "s," as it is, too, in the R.V.

Rom. 1:9 "God is my witness, whom I serve with my *pneuma* in the Gospel of His Son."

Here, *pneuma* is used according to Hebrew Idiom, in which it stands for *reality*, denoting the true essence of the thing; and means whom I really and truly or faithfully serve. Both A.V. and R.V. have a "s" (see Usage No. X.).

Rom. 2:29 "He is a Jew which is one inwardly; and circumcision is that of the heart, in *pneuma*, not *letter*." The A.V. and R.V. both have "s."

Here, "*pneuma*" and "letter" are put by *Metonymy*, for what is internal and external respectively: (as in 2 Cor. iii. 6: which see below). The explanation of this usage is found in James ii. 26: "As the body without (or apart from χωρίς, *chōris*), *pneuma* is dead, so is faith without works." And we may add, so is "Circumcision" (which is the subject here). If it is only external, it is dead; but, if it is internal, and pertains to the heart, then he is a true Jew who is circumcised *inwardly* or *spiritually*, and not merely formally.

Rom. 5:5 "The love of God is shed abroad in our hearts by *pneuma hagion* which is given unto us."

Divine "Love" is one of the "gifts" (or "fruit") which the great Giver, the Holy Spirit, gives (Gal. v. 22). This is another proof that *pneuma hagion* denotes the gift "given unto us," and not the Giver of the gift. Both the A.V. and R.V. insert the article, and use capitals.

Rom. 7:6 There is a great divergence of translation in A.V. text and margin; as well as in the R.V. We therefore give our own rendering which agrees with R.V., and A.V., margin in the main, but avoids the introduction of the words "that" or "to that" of which there is nothing in the Greek:

"But now we (having died) have been discharged from the Law by which we were held fast"; so that we serve in newness of *pneuma*,* and not in oldness of letter."

The expression is adverbial, as in Rom. ii. 29 (see above), and means *spiritual* and in a new manner. In virtue of our new nature, we really and truly serve God, and not formally, as when we served outwardly, with the flesh or our old nature. That service was "religion": this service is Christianity.

Rom. 8:1 Few chapters have suffered more from the loose renderings of *pneuma* than this: for not until we come to verse 16 is the Holy Spirit Himself mentioned.

In verse 1, the last half of the verse must be omitted.† It is similar to the last half of verse 4, and may probably at first have been written by some transcriber in the margin against verse 1, and then afterwards got incorporated with it. It is the fourth passage which all the critical Greek Texts agree to omit as does the R.V.

Rom. 8:2 "For the law of *the pneuma* of life in Christ Jesus hath made me free from the law of sin and death."‡

In this chapter, *pneuma* receives its peculiar Pauline

---

* Both A.V. and R.V. have "s."

† The A.V. of 1611 had a small "s." Current editions have "S." The R.V. omits it.

‡ The A.V. of 1611 had "s." Current editions, and R.V. have "S."

usage; and is put (by *Metonymy*) for *the new nature;* because it is the greatest of the gifts which come of the operation of the Holy Spirit Himself. (See above, Usage No. V.).

The new nature is called "*pneuma*," just as the old nature is called "flesh": because, "as the body (the flesh) without *pneuma* is dead" (Jas. ii. 26), so man, without this real *pneuma*, the new nature, is counted dead before God (Eph. ii. 1, 5) because he is "alienated from the life of God" (Eph. iv. 18).

All men (physiologically) have material flesh and immaterial *pneuma* (Gen. ii. 7). But man is a fallen creature; and is mortal. A new *pneuma* has therefore to be given to him to make him a "partaker of the Divine nature" (2 Pet. i. 4). The saved sinner has this *pneuma* now; but his new body he will not get till resurrection. Then, that body will itself be a *pneuma*-body (see 1 Cor. xv. 44).

As long, therefore, as the believer is in this mortal body ("this body of death," Rom. vii. 24), there must be the conflict between the old nature and new. With the new nature the believer is serving the law of God; and with the old nature, the law of sin (Rom. vii. 25).

This *pneuma* is here called "the pneuma of life"; for it gives, not mortal life (as in Gen. ii. 7), but spiritual life, Divine life, eternal life. And having this, we have been made free from the law of sin; yea, from that death which came by sin.

Rom. 8:4   "That the righteous (requirement, R.V. ordinance) of the law might be fulfilled in us who walk not according to flesh (κατὰ σάρκα, *kata sarka*), but, according to *pneuma*** (κατὰ πνεῦμα, *kata pneuma*). †

---

* There is no article. The A.V. of 1611 and R.V. have " s."
But current editions of A.V. have " S."

† The word here is *not* δικαιοσύνη (*dikaiosunē*), *the attribute of*

The article is not expressed, as it is latent after the preposition; and it is the old nature (the flesh), and the new nature (*the pneuma*), which are spoken of and contrasted. He who has this new nature, walks according to it, and thus fulfils all the " righteous requirements " of the Law, to which he has died in Christ. God regards him as having judicially died when Christ died: (and he is so to "reckon" himself now. Rom. vi. 11), The Law has no power over a dead man (Rom. vii. 4. and 6 marg.); and yet we fulfil all it can righteously require, inasmuch as we walk henceforth in the power of this new nature, or " newness of life": *i.e.*: according to *pneuma*.

Rom. 8:5   (twice) " For they that are according to flesh do mind the things of the flesh; but they that are according to *pneuma* [do mind] the things of *the pneuma*."*
The article with the second *pneuma* is only grammatical, in order to identify it with the former which immediately precedes it.

Rom. 8:6   " For the mind of the flesh [is] death, but the mind of *the pneuma** [is] life and peace."

Not until we have this *pneuma*, or new nature, have we true, real, Divine, eternal " life " ; and not till then can we know what is true " peace." Then we understand the nature of the conflict described in Chap. vii.; and know that, in spite of all that seems to the contrary, "we

---

righteousness, but δικαίωμα (*dikaiōma*), *the righteous thing;* the Context showing what that righteous thing is. In Luke i. 6, Heb. ix. 1, 10 it is the righteous *ordinance* of the Law. In Rom. i. 32 and Rev. xv. 4 it is the righteous sentence or *judgment* of God. In Rom. ii. 26, and viii. 4 it is the righteous *requirement* (R.V., " ordinance ") of the law. In Rom. v. 16 it is the righteous *acquittal* of the Law. In Rom. v. 18, it is the righteous *act*. In Rev. xix. 8 it denotes the righteous *awards given*.

*The A.V. of 1611 and R.V. have "s," but current editions of A.V. have "S."

have peace with God" (Rom. v. 1). Indeed, this very conflict becomes itself the ground of our peace; for it is the surest evidence we can have that we possess the new nature which is God's own "new creation" work within us (2 Cor. iv. 17, Eph. ii. 10); and hence we have not only life, but a life which is peace itself. The Figure *Hendiadys*, "life and peace," is intended to mark this blessed reality of "PEACEFUL life" in the midst of internal conflict; for it puts all the emphasis on the word *peaceful*.

Rom. 8:9 (three times) "Ye are not in [the] flesh, but in [the] *pneuma* ; * if so be that, *pneuma* † *Theou* dwelleth in you. But if any man have not *pneuma*† *Christou*, he is not his" (A.V., "none of his").

Here *Theou* (of God), and *Christou* (of Christ) are the Genitive of *Character*, and mean respectively *Divine pneuma* and *Christ-pneuma*.

Though the flesh is in us, yet we are not reckoned as being in the flesh, our old man having been crucified with Christ (Gal. ii. 20, Rom. vi. 6). We are in *pneuma*, i.e., in the new nature, and in the new creation, if *pneuma* from God dwells in us : i.e., that new nature of which God is the Creator (2 Cor. v. 17, Eph. ii. 10). We might well render this, " Divine nature," in harmony with the statement in 2 Pet. i. 4, which declares that such are "partakers of the Divine nature."

If we have not this *pneuma Christou*—this Christ *pneuma*, we are none of His. Christ had this *pneuma Theou* as the "Son of God": and all who are "sons of God" now are and are joint heirs with Christ, have this same *pneuma*, as He had. This is why it is called *Christ-pneuma*, as is explained in verses 15-17.

---

* A.V. 1611 and R.V. have "s." Current editions of A.V. have "S."

† A.V. 1611 had "s," but current editions with R.V. have "S."

Rom. 8:10   "And, if Christ be in you, the body indeed* [is] dead, on account of sin, but *the pneuma* [is] life on account of righteousness." Christ was delivered and was put to death on account of our sins, but was raised again on account of our justifying, or being declared righteous (Rom. iv. 25).†

That is to say, Christ's death justified His People. When, therefore, He was raised again from the dead, that resurrection was the declaration of it—the Divine promulgation of the decree pronouncing our justification. His resurrection is our receipt, the evidence to us that our debt has been paid and the bond cancelled. His blood was not the receipt, but *the price*. His death was not the receipt, but it was *the payment* of the debt. His resurrection, therefore, is *the receipt for that payment*. Hence, it goes on to state the blessed consequence of this in ensuring our own resurrection.

Rom. 8:11   (twice). "And if *the pneuma* (*i.e.*, the new nature from God, the article being used grammatically to identify this *pneuma* with what has been said about it above) of him that raised up Jesus from among the dead is dwelling in you, He that raised up the Christ (Jesus‡) from among the dead will quicken your mortal bodies

---

*Neither the A.V. nor the R.V. translates this word μέν *(men) indeed*, or *although*.

†The word here is δικαίωσις *(dikaiōsis)*, which denotes the *action* of the judge in declaring or recognising a person as δίκαιος *(dikaios) righteous*.

‡Tischendorf and R.V. add "Jesus." Lachmann puts it in brackets as we have done. These titles are very significant, and are used in all perfection. "Jesus" it was who died. That was the name associated with his humiliation. But it is "Christ," the Messiah (who, as Jesus, had been humbled) who was raised and glorified.

also, on account of His *pneuma** (*i.e.*, the Divine Nature) that dwelleth in you."†

Rom. 8:13   " For if ye are living according to [the] flesh ye must die,‡ but if by *pneuma* (*i.e.*, by the new nature) ye are putting to death by [reckoning according to chap. vi. 11] the deeds of the body, ye will live " (*i.e.*, live again in resurrection life, as the word generally means§).   The A.V. of 1611 and R.V. have "s." Current editions of A.V. have "S."

Rom. 8:14   " For, as many as are led by *pneuma Theou* (*pneuma* of God: *i.e.*, by this new or Divine nature) these are " God's sons."

As many as are led by God's *pneuma*, they are God's sons.

This is not the same *pneuma Theou* as in Matt. xii. 28 ; because there both the context and the article (which is latent after the preposition ἐν, *en*, *by*), show that the Holy Spirit is there meant.   There is no preposition here, and therefore no article is implied : nor does the context admit of the introduction of any new subject different from that which is being dealt with in these verses, 1-15.   (The A.V. of 1611 had a small " s " here ; but the current editions, with R.V., have " S."

Rom. 8:15   (twice). " For ye received not a bondage-*pneuma*, again, unto fear (*i.e.*, with a view to

---

* So the Textus Receptus, with many ancient authorities, followed by the A.V. and R.V. in margin.

† Here again the A.V. of 1611 had a small "s" in both cases, but current editions have a capital "S." The R.V. has the first with "s," and the second with "S."

‡ Greek μέλλετε ἀποθνῄσκειν (*mellete apothnēskein*) *ye are about to die*, *i.e.*, ye will have to die.

§ See Matt. ix. 18. Acts ix. 41. Mark xvi. 11. Luke xxiv. 5, 23. John xi. 25, 26. Acts, i, 3; xxv. 19. Rom. vi. 10; xiv. 9. 2 Cor. xiii. 4. Rev. i. 18; ii. 8; xiii. 14; xx. 4, 5.

making you serve in fear) : but ye received a sonship-
pneuma,* whereby we cry Abba [*i.e.*] 'my Father.'"

Rom. 8:16   (twice).   Now we come to the change
in the usage of *pneuma* in this chapter.   It is most
marked and unmistakable, because in this verse we have
pneuma twice.   The first time it is the Holy Spirit who
is spoken of as the One who, having been the Giver of
this wondrous gift of the *pneuma*, or new nature, now
witnesses with it and through it ; speaking to us, and
communicating with us, through it.

" *The Pneuma* (or Spirit) Himself beareth witness with
our *pneuma*, that we are God's children."

Notwithstanding that both words have the article,
the context makes the sense perfectly clear :—The
Holy Spirit witnesses with the new nature which has
been spoken of in the previous context.   The first article
is demonstrative, showing that the Holy Spirit is the
subject as the Giver; whereas the second is grammatical, identifying it with what has been mentioned
before, as the gift.

The A.V. of 1611 had "s" in both cases ; but the
current Editions, and R.V., have the first " S," and the
second " s."

Rom. 8:23   " We ourselves . . . which have the
first-fruit of *the pneuma*."

This may be the Genitive of *Origin*, and mean the
first-fruit which the Holy Spirit gives, as the Giver; or
it may be the Genitive of *Apposition*, and mean " the
first-fruit, which is *the pneuma*, or the new nature."   The
Holy Spirit, the great Giver, having given us this great
gift, we may look on it as the first-fruit of all that He

---

* The A.V. of 1611 and R.V. have "s" in both cases : but the
current Editions have the first " s " and the second " S."

will do for us, including even the redemption of our body from the grave.

The A.V. of 1611 had " s." But the current Editions with R.V. have " S."

Rom. 8:26   (twice). " Likewise *the pneuma* also helpeth our infirmities : for we know not what we should pray for as we ought : but *the pneuma* itself maketh intercession for us, with groanings which cannot be uttered."

Rom. 8:27   " He that searcheth the hearts knoweth what is the mind of the *pneuma* " : *i.e.*, the Holy Spirit, spoken of in verse 26. The A.V. of 1611 had " s " ; but the current editions with R.V. have " S."

Rom. 9:1   " My conscience bearing me witness with *pneuma hagion :* " *i.e.*, his good conscience was the result of the Holy Spirit's operation. Here A.V. and R.V. have " the Holy Ghost." They insert the article, and use capitals. The A.V. of 1611 had " the holy Ghost."

Rom. 11:8   " God hath given them a *pneuma* of slumber." This is the Genitive of Relation, for sound sleep ; or, as it is expressed in Isa. xxix. 10, " deep sleep " (see under Usage No. VII. above). The A.V. inserts the article, and has a small " s." The R.V. has no article, and uses " s " (" a spirit of stupor ").

Rom. 12:11   " Fervent in *the pneuma*." See the Idiom in Acts xviii. 25 (Usage No. X.). Here both versions have " s."

Rom. 14:17   " Righteousness, and peace, and joy through (in or with) *pneuma hagion*." These are parts of the " fruit of the Spirit," and therefore are called *pneuma hagion*. The A.V. and R.V. insert the article, and use capital letters. See chap. xv. 13 below.

Rom. 15:13 "That ye may abound in hope, through power of *pneuma hagion*." Here it may be the Genitive of Apposition. There is no article with power, so that it would read, "That ye may abound in hope through (or with) power which is *pneuma hagion*." Both versions insert the article, and use capital letters.

Rom. 15:16 "Being sanctified by [the] *pneuma hagion*." Here the article is latent after the preposition ἐν (*en*), by, and therefore it may denote the Holy Spirit. Otherwise, it is the gift that is meant as in other places. Both versions use capital letters.

Rom. 15:19 "Through mighty signs and wonders by power of *pneuma hagion*." The Textus Receptus and A.V. have "*pneuma Theou*," *spirit of God*. But all the Critical Texts with R.V. read *pneuma hagion;* clearly referring to spiritual gifts, or "power from on high." Both versions insert the article, and use capitals.

Rom. 15:30 "Now I beseech you, brethren, by our Lord Jesus Christ, and by the love of *the pneuma*, that ye strive together with me in your prayers to God for me."

Here it is "by," as R.V., not "for the sake of." It is διά (*dia*) with the Genitive, and denotes *by means of.* The context shows (with the use of the definite article) that the Holy Spirit is meant: for the three persons of the Trinity are all mentioned in this one verse.

Both versions have "S."

The "love of the Spirit" is the Genitive of Origin ; and means that this love is the gift of the Spirit, the "love of God," which He, the Spirit, sheds abroad in our hearts. That love would be the means of causing them to pray for the apostle as he desired.

1 CORINTHIANS

1 Cor. 2:4 " My speech and my preaching was not with enticing (marg. *persuasible ;* R.V. text " persuasive ") words of [human*] wisdom, but in demonstration of *pneuma* and power."

Here, both A.V. and R.V. interpolate the article " the," and use a capital " S," though there is no article and no word " holy " in the Greek.   The Figure is clearly, *Hendiadys*, by which two words are used and one thing is meant ; the second noun becoming a superlative adjective. Here, it denotes the powerful gift of Divine wisdom, in contrast with the weakness of human wisdom mentioned in the next verse.   The usage here is the same as in Acts vi. 3, 5, 8, 10.

1 Cor. 2:10 (twice). " But to us God hath revealed [it] by *the pneuma* : † (*i.e.,* by the Holy Spirit), for *the pneuma* searcheth all things, even the deep things of God."   Here it is the Holy Spirit, the Giver and Worker, in operation and manifestation. Both versions rightly have " S."

The context shows that the pronoun "it " should be supplied, and not "them," as the Mystery is the subject. The R.V. has "*it*" in the margin.

1 Cor. 2:11 (twice).   " For what man knoweth the [deep] things of a man save *the pneuma* of a man, which is in him ? even so the [deep] things of God knoweth no man, but *the pneuma* of God."

---

* The word ἀνθρώπινος *(anthrōpinos), human,* is omitted by all the Critical Greek Texts, and R.V.   But it is clearly implied and must be supplied from verses 5 and 13.

† The pronoun " his " (or lit., " of him ") is omitted by L.T.Tr. and R.V.   Alford puts it in brackets.

Here, though we have the article in both sentences, *pneuma* is used, in the first, psychologically ; and the article is used grammatically. Man's *pneuma* is contrasted with God's *pneuma*. Both versions correctly use " s " for the first, and " S " for the second.

1 Cor. 2:12 (twice). " Now we have received not *the pneuma* of the world, but *the pneuma* which is from God, that we might know the things that are freely given to us by God."

Here it is the *gift* of the new nature, which is set in contrast with the natural man, and the rest of the world. It is the spiritual " understanding " of 1 John v. 20; without which we neither *know* (οἶδα *oida*) nor can we *get to know* (γινώσκω, *ginōskō*) the things of God.

The **A.V.** of 1611 and R.V. use " s " in the first case and " S " in the second. But current editions of **A.V.** have " s " in both cases.

1 Cor. 2:13 " Which things we speak also, not with the words which man's wisdom teacheth, but with [those words] taught by *pneuma* [*hagion**] declaring † spiritual things to spiritual men."

Here, it is the Dative plural masculine, and means *to spiritual persons*. The Corinthian Christians were not thus spiritual ; they were " carnal," because they were concerned with the Ecclesiastical bodies of man's

---

* All the Critical Texts, with R.V., omit "*hagion*" (holy). Both A.V. and R.V. insert the article and use capital letters.

† The word συγκρίνω *(sunkrinō)* occurs only here and 2 Cor. x. 12, twice ; (where the reading is doubtful ; κρίνω *(krinō)* being substituted for it in the first occurrence by Tischendorf). It means *to communicate*, *declare*, or *make known*. It is used for the Heb. פָּרַשׁ *(parash)* in Num. xv. 34 ; where it had not been " declared " what was to be done with the man who gathered sticks on the Sabbath. Compare also Gen. xl. 8, 16 ; xli. 12 ; and Lev. xxiv. 12.

making, and were not occupied with the "one body," which God has already made in Christ. Hence they were "carnal" (ch. iii. 1-5); and, therefore, when the Apostle went to Corinth, he could not make known "the Mystery" (so R.V. in ch. ii. 1) or Secret concerning this spiritual body of the Christ, which depends on the great doctrine of Christ and Him RISEN. He could not advance beyond the teaching connected with Christ and Him "crucified." But now, at the time when he writes this Epistle, he is able to reveal the "mystery;" and he does so in chapter xii.

Here, it is the gift, and not the Giver; the gift of Heavenly and Divine wisdom, made known in Spirit-taught words.

1 Cor. 2:14 "The natural (*psychic*) man receiveth not the things of *the pneuma* of God": *i.e.*, the things done, and the words spoken, by the Holy Spirit. Both versions have capitals.

1 Cor. 3:16 " Know ye not that ye are A TEMPLE (Sanctuary or Shrine) of God, and *the pneuma* of God dwelleth among you ?"

The scope of this chapter is the one Body of God's building in contrast with the many bodies, fellowships, or communities, of man's making. These are said to be "carnal." The other is spiritual. When the Holy Spirit is spoken of as indwelling, the word "body," or "temple," is *always in the singular*. Believers are addressed collectively as being in Christ, "builded together for AN HABITA-TION of God through the Spirit" (Eph. ii. 22). This building, being "fitly framed together, groweth unto AN HOLY TEMPLE in the Lord" (*v.* 21).

The argument is here that "if any man defile the temple of God, him shall God destroy: for the temple of God is holy, which temple ye (*plural*) are " (*v.* 17).

The word rendered " defile " means *to mar, to make of none effect by defiling it.**

The " One Body " is marred in the case of those who make other bodies or corporate fellowships. By these the " unity of the Spirit " is made of none effect ; and thus, in a certain sense, (so far as they were concerned), destroyed.

So that, here, it is the Holy Spirit, indwelling the spiritual body of Christ as a whole—and filling the separate members of it with His gifts and by His power.

1 Cor. 4:21   " Shall I come . . . in *a pneuma* of *meekness.*"   This is the Genitive of attribute or character. (See Usage No. VII.) : and means, in a meek spirit ; or, in great meekness.   Both Versions have " s," but A.V. inserts the definite article " the."

1 Cor. 5:3   " I verily, as absent in body, but present in *pneuma.*"   Here the Dative case is used adverbially.   Paul speaks of being absent from them actually and bodily, but with them, in a very real sense, in thought and feeling.

1 Cor. 5:4   " Being gathered together, ye and my *pneuma.*"

Here, again, by *Metonymy* (of the cause), *pneuma* is put for that which is produced by, or emanates from, the man, which is invisible : or, his thought, his instructions on the matter before them :

Or, it may be, by Synecdoche, put for " me " present with you in thought.   Both Versions use " s."

1 Cor. 5:5   " That *the pneuma* may be saved in the day of the Lord Jesus."

---

* The word φθείρω (*phtneirō*) is always translated *corrupt,* except in these two occurrences in this verse. See 1 Cor. xv. 33 ; 2 Cor. vii. 2 ; xi. 3 ; Eph. iv. 22 ; Jude 10 ; Rev. xix. 2. So R.V., except both times in 1 Cor. iii. 17 and Jude 10, where it has *destroy :* but *corrupted* in the margin.

Here pneuma is used psychologically of the *pneuma* of man as distinguished from his "flesh," according to Gen. ii. 7. The *pneuma*, in any case, returns to God at death (Eccles. xii. 7 ; Acts vii. 59) ; but it is reunited to the body in resurrection. Hence the being saved is connected with " the day of the Lord Jesus."

Both Versions use " s."

1 Cor. 6:11 " In the name of the Lord Jesus, and by *the pneuma* of our God." Here, without a doubt, it is the Holy Spirit Himself. Both Versions use capitals.

1 Cor. 6:17 " He that is joined unto the Lord is one *pneuma*," *i.e.*, a member of the spiritual body of Christ. If we are "in Christ," we are "members" (*v.* 15) of His one spiritual body (*v.* 15), and not members of any earthly corporate fellowship. All such are "carnal" (1 Cor. iii. 1-5), and cannot receive the truth of the *One* Body, because they are not in a fit spiritual condition to have the blessed truth of this " Mystery " or Secret made known to them.

Both Versions use " s."

1 Cor. 6:19 " Know ye not that your body is a temple (or *sanctuary*, R.V. marg.) of the *hagion pneuma* in you, which ye have of (or from) God."

Both Versions use capital letters. Here the truth connected with the one spiritual body of Christ (1 Cor. iii. 16) is applied to bodies of individual members of that Body. That One Body is indwelt by One Spirit. The members of it are indwelt by *pneuma hagion ;* for, in spite of the article, it is not the Giver, but the gift which we " have from " Him. Indwelt by His "power from on high," our bodies are like the Sanctuary of old, filled, not with the material or visible Shechinah, or " glory of the Lord," but with *holy pneuma*, spiritual power, and Divine gifts.

1 Cor. 6:20 "Therefore" (this being so, the exhortation is) "glorify God in your body."

All the critical Greek Texts with R.V. omit the clause that follows in Stephens' Text. "And in your *pneuma*, which are God's." According to this it formed no part of the ancient Text. It certainly seems to weaken the whole point of the argument. The scope of the passage is the body. It is not a question of the *pneuma* at all. This is the fifth passage in which the word *pneuma* is omitted.

1 Cor. 7:34 "That she may be holy both as to body and as to *pneuma*." All the critical Greek Texts, with that of the Revisers, add the article in both cases: but the usage here is not affected by it either way; for it is psychological, according to Gen. ii. 7. Both Versions use "s." The R.V. omits the article in the English.

1 Cor. 7:40 "I think also that I have *pneuma Theou*," *i.e.*, Divine spirit, Divine power, Divine inspiration. It refers to the gift of inspiration which he had, and not to the Giver. Compare Rom. viii. 9, 14. Both Versions insert the Article and use capitals.

The word rendered "think" implies the certainty of assured belief. Compare Luke i. 3; x. 36; xii. 40; xvii. 9; xxii. 24. John v. 39. Acts xv. 25, 28, 34; xxvi. 9. 1 Cor. x. 12, etc.

1 Cor. 12:3 (twice). "No man speaking by *pneuma Theou* calleth Jesus accursed:" *i.e.*, no one speaking by the Divine New Nature, with the gift of tongues, thus speaks. By this test they could "try the *pneumata* (spirits)" (*v*. 10).

"No man can say 'Jesus is Lord' but by *pneuma hagion*."

This means much more than merely pronouncing the two words with the lips. Any one can do that; but it means, to call Jesus, " Lord," to confess Him as Lord and Master; to confess ourselves as being His possession, and loving to be under His rule, control, and guidance. No one can do this except by Divine power, " power from high," by *pneuma hagion*, which is the great spiritual gift, given by the Holy Spirit as the Giver. (Compare ch. vii. 40, and Rom. viii. 9, 14.)

The A.V. of 1611 had holy Ghost. But the current editions have Holy Ghost. The R.V. uses capitals in both cases.

1 Cor. 12:4 " There are diversities of gifts, but *the* same *pneuma*." Here we have the Holy Spirit as the Giver of these divers gifts.

We have also further evidence of this supplied by the context: for in verse 4 we have " the Spirit ; " in verse 5, we have "the Lord " (Christ) ; and in verse 6 we have " God " the Father.

The A.V. of 1611 used a " s " here. But the current editions with the R.V. have " S."

1 Cor. 12:7 " But the manifestation of *the pneuma* is given to each man for [the general] profit."

Here, again, it is what is given by the great Giver (the Holy Spirit) as indicated by the context and the article. The A.V. of 1611 had " s." Current editions and R.V. have " S."

1 Cor. 12:8 (twice). " To one is given by *the pneuma* the word of wisdom ; to another the word of knowledge, by *the* same *pneuma*."

Here, as in verse 7, it is the Giver in both cases. The A.V. of 1611 had " s " in both these verses. But current editions, with R.V., have " S."

1 Cor. 12:10   " To another [is given] the discerning of *pneumata*."

Here it denotes, either the discerning of spiritual gifts, or of evil spirits or demons.

Both Versions have " s."

1 Cor. 12:11   " All these worketh *that* one and *the* selfsame *pneuma*, dividing to each one severally as he will."   The A.V. of 1611 had " s."   Current editions, with R.V., have " S."

He is the great Giver of all these spiritual gifts : and He gives them, not as we will, but "AS HE WILL." We are not, therefore, to chide or lash ourselves or others because we or they have not these gifts.   No one can receive any of these gifts, except as " He," the Giver, may be pleased to bestow them.   No one has any " claim " to them ; none can " demand " them ; nor can we establish any right to receive what has never been promised.   If we desire a special gift, we incur a grave responsibility.   May the Giver never give us a gift without at the same time bestowing the grace to use it aright : for our profit, for the good of others, and for His own glory.

1 Cor. 12:13   (twice).   " With one *pneuma* are we all baptized into one body . . . and have all been made to drink* at one *pneuma*."   This seems to be the force of the εἰς (*eis*) ; which, on account of its difficulty in this position is omitted by all the Critical Greek Texts.   We who are baptized *with* one *pneuma*, are all made to drink *at* the same spiritual fountain and streams, to which we are led out (compare Luke xiii. 15).

Here there is no article.   The A.V. of 1611 had " s " in both cases.   Current editions, with R.V., have " S " :

---

* All the Critical Greek Texts and R.V. omit εἰς (*eis*), into.

it cannot mean the Holy Spirit. How can we drink a person, or be baptized with a person?

John truly baptized with *water*. The element of his baptism (which related to the One who was to come) was *material*. But the baptism with which Christ (who is the baptizer*) baptizes, relates to Himself, *who has come*, and, in resurrection is made " a quickening spirit," and has a *spiritual* element in which He baptizes all the members of His body. That body is One. That baptism is *One*. " There is one baptism." (See Eph. iv. 5.) In Religion all is material. In Christianity (which is Christ) all is spiritual. The members of His body are endued (Greek *clothed*) with " power from on high." The future baptism of Israel is to be with spiritual water (Ezek. xxxvi. 24-31): how much more shall our baptism now be with spiritual water. See on John iii. 5, above.

1 Cor. 14:2 " Howbeit, in *pneuma*, he speaketh mysteries " (or secret things). Here, there is no article, and the subject of the whole context is spiritual gifts, and especially the gift of " speaking with tongues." Both Versions have " s."

1 Cor. 14:12 " Forasmuch as ye are zealous of *pneumata*."

Here it is plural; and both the A.V. and R.V. actually translate this " spiritual *gifts*," and put in the margin " Gr. *spirits*," with a small "s"; the word "gifts" in the Text being in italic type. This is conclusive evidence as to the usage of *pneuma* to denote *a spiritual gift*.

1 Cor. 14:14 "If I pray in an [unknown] tongue my *pneuma* prayeth, but my understanding is unfruitful." Both Versions have " s."

---

* Christ did not baptize when on earth; not even with material water (John iv. 2). His baptizing was reserved till after His resurrection, and that, with spiritual water, or *pneuma hagion*.

It is only one who is really born again from above who can really pray. Prayer is the breath of the new nature (as the Word of God is its food). The prayer of the " lips,'' or of the natural man, is not prayer at all. Paul used to pray, as Saul: for he was a Pharisee, and must have " made long prayers " : but when God said of Saul to Ananias (Acts ix. 11), " Behold he prayeth," it was the first time that this could be truly said of him.

1 Cor. 14:15 (twice). " I will pray with *the pneuma* . . . I will sing with *the pneuma*."

Here, again, it denotes the new nature. Both Versions have " s " in both cases.

1 Cor. 14:16 " Else, when thou shalt bless with *the pneuma*."

Here, all the Critical Greek Texts omit the article. But the meaning is the same in either case, as in verse 15. Both Versions have " s."

1 Cor. 14:32 " And prophets' *pneumata* (plural), are subject to [the] prophets."

There are no articles in the Greek. The reference is clearly to the spiritual gifts of the prophets. These were used in subjection to the prophets. Compare verse 12. Both Versions have " s."

1 Cor. 15:45 " The first man, Adam, was made a living soul ($\psi v\chi\acute{\eta}$, *psuchē*): the last Adam [was made] a quickening *pneuma*." Both Versions have " s."

Here, *pneuma* is used of the resurrection body of Christ, which had " flesh and bones," but not " flesh and blood " ; for " flesh and blood " cannot enter into the kingdom of heaven. (See Luke xxiv. 39, and compare 1 Cor. xv. 50).

We have no means of knowing what the first man was, as the creation of God. We have no means of knowing how great was the " Fall," or what the change was which then took place in what had been created. There is no mention of " blood " till after the Fall. That it became very different from the Resurrection body we are told. That it was very different from the first created body is clearly implied.

The resurrection body is a spirit-body ; yet it will not be like either that of angels or demons, which are merely *pneumata* or spiritual beings.

Nor is it like that of human beings. (See under Usage No. XIII.).

To understand what the human body will be when it is raised from the dead, and " changed," and made like unto Christ's risen and glorious body (Phil. iii. 21), we must remember all that we are told about that body.

As the " Son of Man," " born of a woman," Christ was " living soul," and had a human body of " flesh and blood." This was in Incarnation. But in Resurrection He " became life-giving *pneuma*."

The present psychical, "natural," or *human* body of " flesh and blood " has " blood " for the life thereof.* But the *risen* body has no " blood " ; it is " flesh and bones." Instead of " blood," it has *pneuma* for its life. This *pneuma* gives life immortal and eternal to the risen body. Therefore it is called "*life-giving pneuma*" (not life-giving " blood ").

What the " blood " is to the human body, *pneuma* will be to the resurrection body. " Blood " is the life of the human body, and therefore there can be no immortality for the body " except it die " : except it gives up its blood. Hence the necessity of the Saviour's " shedding of blood." This was necessary to the laying down of the life of the " first Adam," so that, in resurrection, He might become—not again " a living soul "—but,

---

* See Gen. ix. 4 ; Lev. xvii 11, 14 ; Deut. xii. 23, etc.

instead, "the second man," " a life-giving *pneuma*," as " the last Adam."

Man, as man, has nothing to give or to get, in "exchange for his life," or "living soul." But for those "in Christ" there will be a blessed and glorious "exchange." This exchange will be "the gift of God"; for "God giveth it a body, as it hath pleased Him" (1 Cor. xv. 38).

As "living soul," man possesses *pneuma* in a material organism ; and food is absolutely *necessary* to preserve and keep up the vital connection and relation. But, in the resurrection body, while it is able to partake of food (Ps. lxxviii. 25, Matt. xxvi. 29, Acts x. 41), the *pneuma* itself will preserve, for ever, this vital connection. Hence it is then called "*life-giving pneuma*." Thus, life-giving pneuma will be to the future resurrection body what blood is now to the present human body.

We know how food is disposed of in the human body, or "living soul." But we know nothing of what becomes of it in the spiritual body which has a *life-giving pneuma*. We know full well that that body will not be more limited in its powers than the human body. We cannot imagine what those wondrous powers will be. We know only what is revealed; and this, only "in part." It is useless, therefore, for us to speculate.

We know that the body, in Gen. ii. 7, had an existence (but not life) apart from *pneuma ;* but only as *formed* clay, or "dust." The *pneuma* also had a separate existence with God before it was breathed into the body. The body is of dust, and to dust it must return. The *pneuma* is Divine, and therefore immortal. At death, man becomes "a dead soul": because the *pneuma*, its life, "returns to God who gave it" (Eccles. xii. 7). See above, under Usage No. VI. Body and *pneuma* united, is called man, or, " a living soul ": but separated in death man becomes "a dead soul."

This very expression is used in Num. ix. 6, 7, 10, in which passages the Hebrew expression " dead soul" is translated " dead body," without a word in the margin to show the English reader that such a serious change has been made. It is actually rendered "body," Lev. xxi. 11 ; Num. vi. 6; xix. 11, 13. The word " soul " is also rendered "dead" in Lev. xix. 28; xxi. 1; xxii. 4. Num. v. 2; vi. 11. Hag. ii. 13, where again, is no intimation that this is the case.

All these passages prove the fact that, at death, which is the separation of spirit and body, man, who had been " a living soul," becomes a " dead soul." And, that it is only in resurrection that the spirit and body are re-united and raised again in the likeness of Christ (Phil. iii. 21). Man becomes, not again a " living soul," but " a spiritual body "; and has " a life-giving pneuma." Hence the vital importance of the doctrine of resurrection ; which is the distinguishing article of the Christian Faith; marking it off as being absolutely distinct from man's " religions," which have no place for resurrection.*

Spirit-beings, like angels or demons, who have never had a material body, are never spoken of as " souls," or called " living soul."

All that we know about the resurrection body, at present, is revealed in 1 Cor. xv. 42-53.

> " It is sown in corruption ;
> It is raised in incorruption :
> It is sown in dishonour ;
> It is raised in glory :
> It is sown in weakness ;
> It is raised in power :

---

* Those not " in Christ " will, of course, be raised for judgment; but not raised in the likeness of Christ's glorious body.

It is sown a natural† (or, animal) body;
    It is raised a spiritual ‡ body.
There is a natural† (or, animal) body,
    There is a spiritual ‡ body.
And so it is written,
    The first man Adam was made a living soul §;
    The last Adam was made a quickening *pneuma.*
Howbeit, That was not first which is spiritual,‡
          But that which is natural (or, animal);†
And afterwards, that which is spiritual.‡
The first man is of the earth, earthy: ‖
    The second man is the Lord from heaven.
As is the earthy,‖
    Such are they also that are earthy;
And as is the heavenly,¶
    Such are they also that are heavenly.¶
And as we have borne the image of the earthy,‖
    We shall also bear the image of the heavenly,¶
Now this I say, brethren,
    That flesh and blood
        Cannot inherit the kingdom of God;

    Neither doth corruption
        Inherit incorruption.
Behold, I show you a mystery (*i.e.*, tell you a secret):
    We shall not all sleep,
        But we shall all be changed,
        In a moment, in the twinkling of an eye, at the
                last trump:
For the trumpet shall sound,

---

† ψυχικόν (*psychikon*) *psychical*, or, *animal* (See Vulgate).
‡ πνευματικόν (*pneumatikon*) *spiritual.*
§ ψυχὴν ζῶσαν (*psychēn zōsan*) *a living soul*, as Gen. ii. 7.
‖ χοϊκός (*choïkos*) *made of dust.*
¶ ἐπουράνιος (*epouranios*) *heav·nly.*

And the dead shall be raised incorruptible
    And we shall be changed.
For this corruptible
    Must put on incorruption,
And this mortal
    Must put on immortality."

1 Cor. 16:18   " For they have refreshed my *pneuma* and yours."

Here, *pneuma* is put, by *Synecdoche* (a part for the whole); *i.e.*, " they have refreshed you and me." The Figure thus points to the *reality* of the " me " and the " you " : *i.e.*, they were refreshed inwardly and truly.

Both Versions have " s."

2 CORINTHIANS

2 Cor. 1:22   " Who hath also sealed us, and given the earnest of (or, which is) *the pneuma* in our hearts."

The sealer and the giver of this earnest or pledge is God (*v.* 21).   He is the Giver.   The earnest of His stablishing is the *pneuma*, or the new nature, which is His great gift.   It is the Genitive of Apposition :— " the earnest which is the *pneuma*."   Both versions have " S."

2 Cor. 2:13   " I had no rest for my *pneuma* " : *i.e.*, in myself.   As in 1 Cor. xvi. 18.   Both versions have " s."

2 Cor. 3:3   " Ye are manifestly declared to be the epistle of Christ ministered by us, written not with ink, but with *pneuma* of the living God."

Here, *pneuma* is used with the Genitive of Origin or source : *i.e.*, their conversion was due, not to human power or wisdom (as a letter is written with the hand of mortal man and with material ink), but to invisible power and grace (Acts vi. 3, 5, 8, 10), and to the power and operation of the living God Himself.   The A.V. of

1611 had " s "—but current editions have " S " with the R.V.

2 Cor. 3:6 (twice). This verse is, perhaps, the one that, more than any other, is dependent on a right interpretation of the word *pneuma*.

" God hath made us able ministers of a (not 'the') new Covenant (as in R.V. not 'Testament' as in A.V.) : not of letter (no article) but of *pneuma* (no article) : for the letter (the article referring back grammatically to the 'letter' just previously mentioned) killeth, but the *pneuma* (*i.e.*, the '*pneuma*' just mentioned) giveth life." Both versions use " s."

What this "*pneuma*" is we are clearly told, but not till the seventeenth verse.

The scope of this whole passage (2 Cor. iii. 6—18) is to show that the Old Covenant, apart from Christ, is like a dead body.

He is the *pneuma*, and the Old Covenant is the body. And, " as the body without *pneuma* is dead" (Jas. ii. 26), so the Old Covenant as contained in the Old Testament is dead without Christ. Compare John vi. 63, and see pages 133, 134, above.

Hence we have the conclusion stated, in verse 17, at the close of the parenthesis :

" Now the Lord (Christ) is the *pneuma* : and where the *pneuma*, the Lord (Christ) is, there is liberty " as well as " life." The article here, in *v.* 17, refers back to the *pneuma* of verse 6.

Thus, *pneuma*, here, is used of Christ. It cannot mean the Holy Spirit : for it would be stating a needless truism to say " The Spirit is the Spirit.' No : it is " the Lord " (Christ) who is the *pneuma* (*i.e.*, the spirit and life ; or the life-spirit, the life-giving spirit) of the Old Testament, as He Himself testified :—

" It is *the pneuma* that quickeneth ; the flesh (*i.e.*, the 'letter,' profiteth nothing ; the words that I (even I) speak unto you, they are *pneuma* and they are life" (John vi. 63).

But there is still the conclusion to be stated, showing how this affects ourselves now.

Pneuma is necessary to life ; and it quickens and gives life to the Old Covenant, which is a dead letter without it.   In verses 17, 18, we are told how *pneuma* is necessary for *liberty* as well as life.

We, now, are not like the children of Israel who looked on Moses' veiled face : but, like Moses himself, we gaze " with unveiled face " on the glory of Christ.   We are in the position of Moses, who removed the veil when he went in before the presence of the Lord ; and, like him, we are changed by the glory on which we gaze.

This is the teaching of verse 18 :

"But we all with unveiled face [like Moses] beholding-as-in-a-mirror the glory of the Lord, are being transformed [as he was] into the same image, from one glory [reflecting] another glory, even as [coming] from (ἀπό, *apo*) [the] Lord, who is [the] *pneuma* " : (*i.e.*, the pneuma referred to in verses 6 and 17.

In these two verses we have the Genitive of Apposition.

In verse 17 it is " the *pneuma* who is "the Lord [Christ]."

In verse 18 it is "the Lord [Christ] who is the *pneuma*."

We have the same great statement put in two different ways, so that there should be no mistake. The argument of the whole context is that Christ is the *pneuma*, the life and light, of the Old Covenant. The Old Covenant apart from Him was dead (*v.* 6).

" We are (the Apostle's argument is) ministers of this

New Covenant, and in ministering it to you we use great boldness of speech (v. 12). We are not like Moses, who put a veil over his face when he spoke to the people: we use no veil when we speak to you: but we are like Moses when he went in to speak to the Lord. Our faces are unveiled; and, gazing on that glory of Christ, we, like him, are being changed by it; our faces reflect it on you.

In proportion as we are occupied with Christ and His glory, we "are being changed," as Moses' face was changed. The glory which Moses beheld began to change him : and when "we shall see Him as He is" we, too, shall be altogether changed. Our bodies will be made like His own glorious body (1 John iii. 2 ; Phil. iii. 21).

Meanwhile, "beholding Him, we are transformed." The glory which comes (or emanates) from (ἀπό, *apo, away from*) Him who is *pneuma* changes or transforms us "by the renewing of our mind" (Rom. xii. 2).*

Just as, when we look into an Eastern mirror (of polished metal), *we* see ourselves, but *others* see the reflection of the shining metal on our face ; so we, beholding (as in a mirror)† the glory that emanates from (ἀπό, *apo, away from*) Him, have that glory reflected on us. Moses "wist not that the skin of his face shone." And, though we may not see the effect of our occupation with Christ on ourselves, others will see it ; and will "take knowledge of us that we have been with Jesus" our Lord.‡

* The only other place where the word rendered "trans-figure" occurs, except in the Gospel account of the Trans-figuration.

† "Beholding-as-in-a-mirror" is represented by only one word in the Greek, κατοπτριζόμενοι *(katoptrizomenoi)*.

‡ And on the other hand, "if we say that we have no sin" we may "deceive ourselves," but we cannot thus deceive other people.

Thus, in this verse 6, we have *pneuma* twice; and each time the usage is psychological. Both versions use " s."

2 Cor. 3:8 "How shall not the ministration of *the pneuma* be rather glorious"? Here the usage of *pneuma* is again psychological, as in verse 6; and the use of the article with it is grammatical, referring back to the *pneuma* in that verse. Both versions have " s."

This verse (8) is in the parenthesis, already referred to above, which extends from verse 7 to verse 16 (inclusive); and we must give the translation, as required by the scope, which is determined by the Structure.

The Structure of the whole Epistle shows that ch. iii. 1—vi. 10 has the *Ministry of Paul* for its subject: and that ch. iii. 6-18 gives its character, as being the *New Covenant.*

This *Ministry of the New Covenant* (iii. 6-18) is set forth in four members, thus:

A | B | iii. 6. *Pneuma* necessary for LIFE.

   C | 7-16. How *pneuma* changes the Old Covenant.

   B | 17. *Pneuma* necessary for liberty.

   C | 18. How *pneuma* changes us.

The second member C (ch. iii. 7-16), stands by itself, as a parenthesis; the subject of which is:

HOW PNEUMA CHANGES THE OLD COVENANT.

This subject is two-fold. *Pneuma* not only gives *life,* but it brings into *liberty.*

D | E | 7-11. *Pneuma* gives LIFE. (Statement of the Facts).

   E | 12-16. *Pneuma* brings into LIBERTY. (Application of the Facts).

We will present our Translation of verses 7-11 in full, in the form of the Structure:—

How "pneuma" changes the Old Covenant by giving
it LIFE

⟨Expansion and Translation of " B." (Ch. iii. 7-11)
The Statement of the Facts

E | F¹ | 7. THE OLD COVENANT.] "**If, however, the ministration of** [that which inflicted] **DEATH, engraved in writing on stones, came** (ἐγενήθη) **with glory (so that the children of Israel could not gaze on the face of Moses, on account of the glory of his face), which** [glory] **is being annulled** (or superseded):

G¹ | 8. THE NEW COVENANT.] **Will not the ministration of the pneuma** [that gives LIFE] **be** (established, ἔσται) **in glory?**

F² | 9-. THE OLD COVENANT.] "**For if the ministration of** [that which pronounced] **CONDEMNATION** [was with] **glory,**

G² | -9. THE NEW COVENANT.] "**Much rather doth the ministration of** [that which gives] **RIGHTEOUSNESS exceed in glory.**

F³ | 10-. THE OLD COVENANT.] "**For even that which was made glorious had no glory at all in this respect** (*i.e.*, in inflicting DEATH),

G³ | -10. THE NEW COVENANT.] **On account of the surpassing glory** [of giving LIFE.]

F⁴ | 11-. THE OLD COVENANT.] **For if that which is being annulled** [came] **by means of glory** (διὰ δόξης, *dia doxēs*),

G⁴ | -11. THE NEW COVENANT.] **Much more that which remains** [will remain] **in glory** (ἐν δόξῃ, *en doxē*)."

In these members it will be seen that the Old Covenant and the New Covenant are contrasted in several respects, in alternate statements.

A similar alternation is followed in

The Application of the Facts

(Expansion and Translation of "*B*," ch. iii. 12-16).

E | H¹ | 12. " Therefore, having a hope like this, we use much boldness [or liberty] in speaking,

   I¹ | 13-. "(And do not act as Moses did who [when he spoke to the people] used to put a veil over his face, so that the children of Israel should not gaze on it),

H²- | 13. "[For we speak] with a view to the end [*viz.*, Christ] of that which is being annulled.

   I² | 14-. "Yea, their minds were hardened: (for to this very day, during the reading of the Old Covenant, the same veil remains unlifted) ;

H³ | -14. "because it is by Christ that it is being annulled.

   I³ | 15. "Yea, to this day, whenever Moses is read, a veil lies over their hearts ;

H⁴ | 16. " but when it [the mind (*v.* 14-) or heart of the nation] shall have returned to the Lord, the veil will be withdrawn."

The whole of this argument is the application and the illustration of the Old Testament history recorded in Exodus xxxiv. 29-35.

(29) "And it came to pass, when Moses came down from Mount Sinai* with the two tables of Testimony in Moses' hand, when he came down from the mount, that

---

* This was the *seventh* and last descent of Moses from the Mount.

Moses wist not that the skin of his face shone while he
talked with him (God). (30) And when Aaron and all
the children of Israel saw Moses, behold, the skin of his
face shone; and they were afraid to come nigh him.
(31) And Moses called unto them; and Aaron and all
the rulers of the congregation returned unto him: and
Moses talked with them. (32) And afterward all the
children of Israel came nigh: and he gave them in commandment all that the LORD had spoken with him in
Mount Sinai. (33) And [until*] Moses had done
speaking with them, he put a veil on his face. (34) But
when Moses went in before the LORD to speak with him,
he took the veil off, UNTIL he came out. . . . (35)
And the children of Israel saw the face of Moses, that
the skin of Moses' face shone: and Moses put the veil
upon his face again, UNTIL he went in to speak with
him."

The word ἐτίθει (*etithei*) in verse 13 is the *Imperfect*
tense, and may be best translated *used to put*. It
refers to the habit of Moses, whenever he spoke to the
People.

We are not told how long this practice continued;
but there is nothing to show us that it was ever dis-
continued.

Moses' face is put by The Figure *Metonymy* for the
Old Covenant. The People could not look on his face, for
there was a veil between. So now, with the Old
Testament, there is a veil between it and the eyes of the
heart (Eph. i. 18, R.V.); consequently its real glory
(Christ) cannot be seen.

The conclusion of the subject, which was stated in
verse 6, is taken up again (after the parenthesis)
in the significant words in verse 17;

---

* The word " until " must be supplied from verses 34 and 35.

2 Cor. 3:17 (twice). In this verse *pneuma* is used twice; both times of Christ. " Now the Lord (Christ) is that *pneuma* [which thus gives life to the Old Covenant]; and, where the pneuma [that is to say] the Lord is, there is liberty." The Genitive is the Genitive of Apposition. See above, under verse 6. He is *the pneuma* of that " body" (or " letter "). And, without Him, it is itself dead, and ministers only condemnation and death to all who are under it.

The A.V. of 1611 had " s " in the first case, and " S " in the second. But the current editions, with R.V., have " S " in both clauses.

2 Cor. 3:18 " But we all with unveiled face, beholding-as-in-a-mirror the glory of the Lord, are being changed into the same image, from one glory [reflecting] another glory, even as [coming] from (ἀπό, *apo*, *away from*) the Lord who is [the] *pneuma*." The Genitive is the Genitive of Apposition. See above, under verse 6. The A.V. of 1611 had " s." But the current editions, with R.V. have " S."

2 Cor. 4:13 " We having the same *pneuma* (or spiritual gift) [which is] faith," *i.e.*, the Genitive of Apposition : and *pneuma* is used of the spiritual gift of faith. " We having the same spiritual gift [*i.e.*, faith]" : for " faith " is one of the Spirit's gifts. (1 Cor. xii. 8, 9). Both versions have " s."

2 Cor. 5:5 " God, who hath given us the earnest, [which is,] *the pneuma*." Here, again it is the Genitive of Apposition ; and, even though the article is used, it refers back to the original gift of this earnest in Acts ii. 4 and elsewhere. Both Versions have " S."

As human beings, we all have *pneuma* (psychologically), according to Gen. ii. 7: but the gift of the new nature is the assurance, " the earnest " or pledge, that

God will raise us from the dead. Resurrection is the one subject of 2 Cor. v. 1—9. Here, while in this tabernacle we groan, and are "absent from the Lord." We do not wish to be "unclothed" and thus have no body at all : therefore we earnestly "desire to be clothed upon with our house which is from heaven"; *i.e.*, with our resurrection body ; and thus, in it, to be "present with the Lord."

The New Nature which God has given us, is the "earnest" of that resurrection life which Christ is pledged to give us in resurrection ; and which we shall then enter upon in the reality of all its glory, and have and enjoy its eternal fruition.

2 Cor. 6:6 " In all things approving ourselves as the ministers of God (*v.* 4) . . . by pureness, by knowledge, by long-suffering, by kindness, by *pneuma hagion*."

This "power from on high" is thus one of the evidences of ministerial calling.

Both the A.V. and R.V. insert the article here, and use capital letters. The R.V. has a note which reads "Or, *Holy Spirit* : and so throughout this book." It is "so" if it refers to the absence of the article ; but not "so" if it refers to the use of capital letters.

2 Cor. 7:1 "Let us cleanse ourselves from all filthiness of flesh and *pneuma*." Here both A.V. and R.V. have a small "s": and naturally ; for, how can there be any "filthiness" of the Holy Spirit ? But why not, we ask, exercise the same discrimination in other passages ? Why confine the "s" merely to a few places ?

There is no article, either with "flesh" or "spirit." The expression "flesh and spirit" is put by *Metonymy* for human nature ; but here, by *Synecdoche* (a part for the whole) for the whole person—that which is visible and that which is invisible. As we use " body and soul," or " flesh and bones," for the whole person, so we say " mind and body " as denoting the physical and intellectual powers.

2 Cor. 7:13 "The more joyed we for the joy of Titus, because his *pneuma* was refreshed by you all": *i.e.*, Titus himself was refreshed, as the body is refreshed outwardly. Compare Rom. xv. 32, and 1 Cor. xvi. 18; where we have the same thing expressed in other words   Both versions have " s."

2 Cor. 11:4 " If he that cometh is preaching another Jesus, whom we did not preach; or if ye are receiving a different *pneuma*, which ye did not receive; or a different gospel, which ye did not accept [from us] ; ye are doing well in bearing with him." Both versions have " s."
The scope is that they listened to false teaching, but questioned that of the Apostle. They accepted some teacher who had come in his own name, but questioned Paul, notwithstanding he had a Divine commission.
Evil angels or demons *teach* by their mediums (1 Tim. iv. 1, 2) ; and their teachings were then rife, as they are to-day. There is great need for this " spiritual gift " of the " discerning of spirits " (1 Cor. xii. 10) of which he had written to them.
" Another Jesus " is preached to-day : and " spirits " are received which teach very differently from the teaching of the Holy Spirit. But many Christians " bear with them " and get on " well " with them, and do not discern the difference.
Evil spirits are abroad in the earth ; and, as some are " more wicked " than others, some also must be *less wicked* than others. Some teach foul and unclean things ; others teach doctrines that sound so good, and appear

so fair, and seem so holy, that many are deceived by them ; and hesitate even to judge them, though they " discern " them sufficiently to be suspicious of them. If the Lord speaks of " this kind " of spirits (Matt. xvii. 21), there must be *other kinds*. Another " kind " is spoken of in Acts xvi. 17 : where one of them actually endorsed Paul's own teaching, in order to mar his work by tempting him to accept its co-operation. This it did, working through " a certain damsel," for many days. But Paul, when he saw it, was " grieved."* To-day such help is readily accepted, and so long as it sounds " good," and seems fair and holy, God's servants are misled and deceived. There is little or no trying of the spirits as to whether they be of God : hence the warning, not to believe them, is unheeded. (1 John iv. 1.)

If Satan transfigures himself into " an angel of light," it is " no great marvel if his ministers transfigure themselves as ministers of righteousness." (2 Cor. xi. 14, 15). These words refer to solemn realities ; and these ministers are spirits, as well as human beings. Their ministry looks like " light," and it looks like " righteousness." But it is really only darkness ; and the end of both shall be " according to their works " (*v.* 15). They are well-called " misleading "† spirits." (1 Tim. iv. 1).

2 Cor. 12:18 " Walked we not (Titus and himself) in the same *pneuma ?* "

Here *pneuma* is put by *Metonymy* for *mind*, and for that which is internal, in contrast with the next sentence,

---

* The word διαπονεῖσθαι (*diaponeisthai*) occurs only here and Acts iv. 2, and implies *feeling constant* (or, *repeated*) *annoyance*.

† Since 1611 " seducing " has come to be used of one particular form of deception, or misleading.

which refers to what is outward : "walked we not in the same steps ? "

The A.V. has a small " s." The R.V. an " S."

2 Cor. 13:14 " The communion of *the hagion pneuma*."

Here, the context, and the use of the Article, leave us in no doubt that the Holy Spirit is meant. Both Versions rightly use Capitals.

GALATIANS

Gal. 3:2 " Received ye *the pneuma (i.e.,* the new nature) by the works of the law, or by the hearing of faith ?" This is clear from the next verse. The A.V. of 1611 had " s." Current Editions and R.V. have " S."

Gal. 3:3 " Are ye so foolish ? Having begun in (or, by) *pneuma*, are ye now being perfected by *flesh ?* Both Versions insert the article and have " S." But there are no articles in the Greek ; and the two nouns " *pneuma* " and " flesh " are in the Dative case. The new nature is being contrasted with the old nature.

Having begun with the knowledge that the new nature was the gift of God, they were trying to improve the flesh : forgetting that " that which is born of the Spirit is spirit, and that which is born of the flesh is flesh."

This is the great truth of John iii. 6 : according to which the flesh cannot be converted or changed into spirit. There is therefore great necessity for this correction. The doctrine laid down in the Epistle to the Romans had been departed from ; and the correction is given in this Epistle to the Galatians.

How many Christians to-day have begun by possessing this new nature ; but from ignorance of, or from ignoring, this great doctrine of John iii. 6, are seeking to make the flesh perfect by mortifying it ? The only way of putting the flesh to death is by *reckoning* that it was "crucified with Christ" (Rom. vi. 6, 11, Gal. ii. 20), that we "died in Christ." It is "senseless" (or foolish) to treat and deal with a dead thing as though it were alive.

The *new nature* is "perfect," and cannot sin (1 John v. 18, and compare iv. 7; v. 1 and 4) ; while the *old nature* is evil, and cannot but sin (Rom. viii. 6, 7. Jas. iv. 4). The one is the work of the Spirit ; and is, and remains, spirit : the other belongs to the flesh ; and is, and remains, flesh. It cannot be changed into spirit, or be improved. The question, therefore, is : If, then, ye have begun on this foundation of the new nature, why are ye now seeking to make the flesh perfect ? In other words : If ye have been justified by *grace*, why are ye seeking to be sanctified by *works* ?

Gal. 3:5 "He that ministered to you *the pneuma* and worketh miracles (*i.e.*, he that ministered to you, or was the means of your receiving that greatest of all spiritual gifts ; and manifested the lesser gift of working miracles) doeth he it by the works of the law, or by the hearing of faith ?" The use of the article is grammatical, referring to the previous references to *pneuma*. Both versions use "S."

Gal. 3:14 "That we might receive the promise of *the pneuma*." Here it is the Genitive of the Agent : *i.e.* : "the promise made by the Holy Spirit" : or it is the Genitive of Possession, and means "the Spirit's promise." Christ was the "seed promised" by spiritual communication to Abraham. God's "promise" of Gen. xv., &c., is, in the following context, set in contrast with the Law. That promise was Abraham's

" seed "* which was confirmed by God in Christ. Both versions have " S."

Gal. 4:6 " Because ye are sons, God hath sent forth *the pneuma* of his Son into your hearts, crying, Abba, *i.e.*, My Father." Current editions of A.V., with R.V. have " S."

The article is used here; and it refers to the gift of the " sonship-spirit " spoken of in Rom. viii. 15 : *i.e.*: having been made sons, we have, as a spiritual gift, the same sonship-*pneuma* which God's Son has; for we are joint-heirs with Him (Rom. viii. 17).

Gal. 4:29 " He that was born according to flesh persecuted him that was born according to *pneuma*." The same as in Rom. viii. 1, 4, 5. Both versions have " S."

Gal. 5:5 " For we, by *pneuma*, wait for the hope of righteousness, by faith "; *i.e.*, " faith " is one of the gifts of the Spirit. There is no article here; and it is the Spirit's gift of *faith* that is meant, not Himself, the Giver. The A.V. of 1611 had " s." Current editions, with R.V., have " S."

Gal. 5:16 " This I say then, Walk by *pneuma* " (there is no article) : *i.e.*, Walk spiritually, or according to the new nature; and then ye will not fulfil the lust of the flesh (or the old nature). The A.V. of 1611 had " s." It and the R.V. now have " S." Both add the article (R.V. " by the Spirit ").

---

* The Law was given 430 years after this "*promise*" of the seed (Ex. xii. 40, Gal. iii. 17); but 400 years after the fulfilment of the promise in the actual *birth* of " the seed " (Gen. xv. 13, Acts vii. 6).

That promise was unconditional; for God was only " one " party (Gal. iii. 20). The Law was conditional; for there were two parties (Gal. iii. 19), and one of them, Israel, failed. God's covenant was, therefore, a " promise"; which must stand; and it was made by spiritual communication.

Gal. 5:17 (twice). The same as v. 16. It is not till the new nature is given that there can be conflict. Till then, the peace of death reigns. The moment the new nature is given, that moment conflict begins. We find we cannot do all the good things the new nature would have us do; and, thank God, we find also that we cannot do many of the evil things our old nature would have us do. The A.V. of 1611 used " S " for the first, and " s " for the second. Current editions, and R.V. use " S " in both cases.

Gal. 5:18 " But if ye be led by *pneuma* (your new nature) ye are not under law." (As is stated also in Rom. viii. 4). The A.V. of 1611 had " s." Current editions and R.V. have " S." Both insert the article " the."

Gal. 5:22 " The fruit of *the pneuma* " (*i.e.*, the fruit or spiritual gifts of the great Giver, the Holy Spirit), are love, joy, peace," etc. Here, the context distinguishes —by the article with both Spirit and the " fruit "— His spiritual gifts. The A.V. of 1611 had " s." Current editions and R.V. have " S."

Gal. 5:25 (twice). " If we live by *pneuma*, by *pneuma* let us also walk "; as in Rom. viii. 1, 13. Both Versions add the article " the," and use capital letters in both clauses of this verse.

Gal. 6:1 " Brethren even if a man has been overtaken in some transgression, ye, the spiritual [ones] restore such an one in a *pneuma* of meekness; considering thyself, lest thou also be tempted."*

Here *pneuma* is put by Metonymy for the effect of the action of the new nature; and means *meekly* or *with meekness*; which will necessarily be the case if there be this consideration of one's self.

* Both versions have " s."

Alas! alas! How greatly needed is this Divine precept to-day.

The word "Brethren" at the head of the precept is intended to remind us that all are only equally weak, sinful, fellow-servants; and that this fact should dispose us to listen to, and heed, the solemn admonition that follows.

How great is the contrast presented, practically, to-day: and this not merely in cases of actual transgression, but in cases of difference of opinion in the interpretation of Scripture.

This, with many Brethren, is treated as being of far greater importance than honesty in business transactions. Great latitude is shown in matters of that kind, but woe be to those who dare hold honestly a different view of a passage of God's Word.

The conduct of some "Brethren" to-day seems as though they read this verse as if it were written : ' If a man be overtaken in a fault—persecute such an one, cast him out, hound him down; in a spirit of bitterness, not considering thyself!'

Gal. 6:8   (twice).   "He that soweth to *the pneuma* shall of *the pneuma* reap life everlasting"

Here, by the Figure *Ploké*, the first *pneuma* is used of the new nature according to which we sow (or walk); while the second refers to the Holy Spirit Himself, who is the Giver of life everlasting.

The A.V. of 1611 had " s " in both clauses. Current editions with R.V. have " S."

Gal. 6:18   "The grace of our Lord Jesus Christ be with your *pneuma*."

Here *pneuma* is put by *Synecdoche* (*i.e.*, a part for the whole) for the whole person. The clause reads : " The grace of our Lord Jesus Christ be with you," or " with yourselves" (*pl.*).

Both versions have " s " here.

EPHESIANS

Eph. 1:13 " In whom (Christ) ye also [were allotted an inheritance] on hearing the true word of the gospel of your salvation : in whom [Christ] on believing also, ye were sealed [by the Father] with the promised *pneuma* (Lit., *the pneuma* of the promise)—*the hagion*." Both Versions use " S."

The first occurrence of *sealing* is in John xi. 27 and it is attributed to the Father. This gives us the key to this sealing in Ephesians. It is the fulfilment of "the promise of the Father " (Lu. xxiv. 49, Acts i. 9).

There is nothing about " after " in the Greek; either "after that ye heard," or " after that ye believed." It is merely the participle (one word) in both cases, and should be rendered as above : " on hearing " and " on believing "; or "when ye heard," and "when ye believed."

The articles are used here : but the words " *pneuma* " and " *hagion* " are separated (in the Greek) by the words " of the promise"; which looks as though the Father was the Sealer, sealing them with *pneuma*, by the bestowal of the new nature, and with other spiritual gifts which the Gentiles received, as well as the Jews. The Jews are mentioned in verse 11 (" we "); and the Gentiles, in verse 13 (" ye "). Both had been allotted the same inheritance in Christ ; and the earnest or pledge of it (*v.* 14) was the promised gift of *pneuma hagion*, which had been promised by the Father, and is hence, called the promised *pneuma*.

Eph. 1:17 And that He may " give unto you *pneuma* [that is to say] wisdom and revelation in [the] full knowledge of him." The A.V. of 1611 had "S." Current editions and R.V. have "s." The A.V. has the English definite article. The R.V. has "a spirit."

It is the full knowledge (ἐπίγνωσις) *epignōsis;* (not merely γνῶσις, *gnōsis, knowledge*) of God, that is prayed for us here. This must be the gift of *revealed wisdom.* And this revealed wisdom is *pneuma, i.e.,* a spiritual gift (as is implied in verb "give.")

The Figure is *Hendiadys,* and means, "wisdom, yea, —Divinely revealed wisdom." The Genitive is the Genitive of Apposition, and explaining what the special spiritual gift is, that is prayed for (compare Acts vi. 3, "*pneuma* and wisdom.")

Eph. 2:2 "*The pneuma* that now worketh in the children of disobedience."

Here, "*the pneuma*" being in the Genitive must be connected not with "the prince," but with the sphere of his authority (ἐξουσία, *exousia*) viz., *the jurisdiction.* (Compare Lu. xxiii. 7 and 2 Kings xx. 13), *of the air: i.e.:* the lower atmospheric air; the sphere in which man lives and breathes.

Eph. 2:18 "Through him (Christ) we both (Jew and Gentile) have access by one *pneuma* unto the Father."

Here, though there is no article, the context shows that the Holy Spirit is meant. The article is latent after the preposition, and is not required by the grammar.

Both Versions have "S."

Eph. 2:22 In whom (Christ) ye also are being built together for a habitation of God by [the] *pneuma.* Both Versions have "S." The Holy Spirit is the builder of this holy temple for a habitation of God.

HALF PRICE BOOKS

EST. 1972

Half Price Books #061
3757 William Penn Highway
Monroeville, PA 15146
412-856-1949

1-27-22 1:48 PM
tore #0061 / Cashier EPow061 / Reg 2
ale # 380348

SALE TRANSACTION

ingdom Authority: Taking Do 320450445U
  @7.99   Markdown   -4.99 $3.00
ow Sovereign Is Your God? 320773498U
  @6.99   Markdown   -3.99 $3.00

Items in Transaction

ubtotal $6.00
ales Tax (7.0% on $6.00) $0.42
OTAL $6.42

AYMENT TYPE
ISA 7777 $6.42

hanks for shopping at Half Price Books!

H 0 2 0 0 6 1 0 0 2 3 8 0 3 4 3 1

There is no article ; but it is latent after the preposition, and is not required by the grammar.

Eph. 3:5   " It (the Mystery) was lately made known unto his holy apostles and prophets by [the] *pneuma.*" It will be found that *νῦν (nun)*, with the Aorist, in the New Testament, means what we express by "*just now*" or "*lately*," as distinct from *now* at this time.

Here it is the Holy Spirit. Although there is no article (see under ch. ii. 22 above) it is latent after the preposition.

He is the great revealer of this secret, and it was was revealed to the New Testament "apostles and prophets" (see ch. iii. 5). Both Versions have " S."

Eph. 3:16   " That he (the Father) would grant you, according to the riches of his glory (*i.e.*, his glorious riches), to be strengthened with might by *the pneuma* of Him (*i.e.*, His Spirit), in the inner man " (*i.e.*, in the new nature).

Here it is again the Giver of all power and might, the Holy Spirit who is meant. The article being used as well as the preposition διά (*dia*), *by means of*, shows that He is emphatically meant. Both Versions have " S."

Eph. 4:3   " Endeavouring to keep the unity of *the pneuma* : " * *i.e.*, the spiritual unity already effected by God in His having made us the members of the one spiritual body. It is the Genitive of Origin. We do not read of ' the unity (ἑνότητα, *henotēta*†) of the body,' which is so often spoken of, but " the unity of the spirit.' This unity is already made ; and that which we have to

---

* Both Versions have " S."

† The word occurs only here and in verse 13 ; and refers, not to the unity of the one faith, but to the *unity* of the spirit ; *i.e.*, the bond in which the faith and the full knowledge ἐπίγνωσις, *epignosis*) of God binds all the members of this spiritual body.

do is to "keep" it and guard it with diligence. It is not a *corporate* unity which *we* have to *make*; but a spiritual unity which we have diligently to "keep," preserve, and guard.

It is made by the Holy Spirit Himself.

According to the next occurrence of the word *pneuma*, we learn that the body itself is "one." ἕν (*hen*) one. To make any other "body," therefore, or to form any corporate union or "fellowship," and to call it by any other name, is to make a "schism in the body"; and to destroy (for those who make it) the spiritual unity, so far as they are concerned. That unity has been already made by the Holy Spirit. That which is done or effected by Him is spiritual (John iii. 6, pneuma); and our business is to keep watch and guard over, and preserve, that "unity of the spirit."

To do this there is one requisite which is absolutely essential. It is given in the previous verses. The injunction does not commence with the word "Endeavouring." This participle is dependent on a previous statement.

The subject is "His calling" of us (verse 1, compare ch. i. 18):

"I therefore, the prisoner of the Lord, beseech you that ye walk worthily of the calling (i. 18) wherewith ye were called,

> with all lowliness
> and meekness,
> with long suffering,
> forbearing one another in love.

Giving diligence to KEEP the spiritual unity [of the spirit], in the bond of peace." Only by the strict observance of these solemn injunctions can that spiritual union of the members with one another in Christ be preserved and maintained in peace.

What this "lowliness" means is shown in Phil. ii. 3, "in lowliness of mind let each esteem other better than themselves." It does not say 'nearly as good,' or 'as good,' but "BETTER than themselves." How difficult then must be the duty! How necessary must be this *diligence!* How earnest must be this exhortation!

If there be not this mutual humility and meekness, mutual long suffering, mutual forbearing of one another, and the exhibition of mutual love, there will be no real spiritual unity, and no peace.

Instead of "one Body," there will be many Bodies; gendered by pride, and fostered by and exhibiting envy, hatred, malice, and all uncharitableness.

It is just in this point that the saints have failed from the beginning, and all through the ages.

The central truth of Ephesians, the one Body, having been lost, *practical* errors necessarily ensued through not holding the truth concerning the members; and *doctrinal* errors crept in through "not holding the Head."

The former is reproved in Philippians. The latter is corrected in Colossians.

Hence it is that we have the injunction of Eph. iv. 1-3, 30-32 enforced in such precepts and examples as are given in Phil. i. 27; ii. 1-4, 8, 20, 26, 30; iii. 16; iv. 2.

The exhortations of Eph. iv. 30-32 show that the special grieving of the Holy Spirit of God is caused by not holding and manifesting this spiritual unity of the One Body.

Eph. 4:4 "There is one body, and one *pneuma*." The A.V. of 1611 had "s." Current editions and R.V. have "S."

As all the members of the human body are held together in one organism, and that body is kept corporately one, by one *pneuma*, which preserves each of its members in life (Jas. ii. 26), so the members of the one spiritual body are held together in one, and by one *pneuma* they are preserved, in spiritual union with the Head, in heaven, who is the life of each member.

This body is spiritual: because no living body can be complete without the head; and, as the Head of this body is in heaven, the unity must of necessity be spiritual. Hence the sin (to say nothing of the folly) of attempting to form a corporate body; and of actually calling it "the unity of the body," when God calls it "the unity of *the pneuma*."

Eph. 4:23 "Be renewed in *the pneuma* [that is to say] your mind." (Lit., "*pneuma* of your mind").

Here, it is the Genitive of Apposition; and this defines what is meant by *pneuma* here. It is called "mind," as in Rom. vii. 25: *i.e.*, the spiritual mind, or the new nature. Both Versions have "s."

Eph. 4:30 "Offend not *the pneuma*, the holy, of God, by Whom ye were sealed." Both Versions have "S."

Here there can be no doubt as to the Holy Spirit's being meant. And the meaning is *offend* as in Rom. xiv. 15 (compare *v.* 21), or *anger* as in Gen. iv. 5; xlv. 5; 1 Sam. xxix. 4; 2 Kings xiii. 19; Neh. v. 6; Est. i. 12; ii. 21; Isa. viii. 21; Jonah iv. 1, 4, 9.

The two verses that follow (*vv.* 31, 32) show what this offending the Holy Spirit is. It is not by defects in our general walk as Christians; but in our special failure in not manifesting the kindness, and meekness, and tenderness, and forbearance, which are requisite for the preservation of the spiritual unity of the One Body.

Eph. 5:9 Here, all the critical Greek Texts and R.V. read φωτός (*phōtos*) *of light*, instead of πνεύματος (*pneumatos*) *of spirit*.

This is the sixth of the nine passages where all the Editors say *pneuma* is to be omitted.* And the effect of the omission is to cause verses 8 and 9 to read:

" Walk as children of light: (for the fruit of the light consists in all goodness and righteousness and truth) proving what is well-pleasing unto the Lord."

Eph. 5:18,19 " Be not drunk with (or by) wine wherein is excess; but be filled by [the] *pneuma*; speaking to yourselves (R.V. one another: marg., *to yourselves*) in psalms, and hymns, and spiritual songs, singing and making melody in your heart to the Lord."

It is a grammatical law that the verb *to fill* ($\pi\lambda\eta\rho\acute{o}\omega$, *pleroō*) takes after it (or governs) more than one case of the noun, in order to distinguish, and to enable us to identify (1) the *thing filled*, (2) the *material* that fills it, and (3) the *agent* or instrument that effects the filling.

(1) It takes the *Accusative* case of the thing filled:

(2) It takes the *Genitive* case of the matter with which the thing is filled.† The idiom being, to be filled *of* a thing; whereas the English idiom is, filled *with a* thing.

(3) It takes the *Dative* case of the means used to accomplish the filling; or of the instrument or agent that fills.

Sometimes the preposition ($\grave{\epsilon}\nu$, *en*) *by* or *through* is used in addition to the Dative case (as here), in order to emphasize this agent.

A few examples will serve to make this clear:

Matt. xxiii. 32. " Fill ye up then the measure (Acc.) of your fathers."

---

*The other eight are Luke ii. 40; ix. 55. Acts xviii. 5. Rom viii. 1. 1 Cor. vi. 20. 1 Tim. iv. 12. 1 Pet. i. 22. 1 John v. 7.

† Sometimes it takes the Accusative, according to *Hebrew* idiom; but never the Dative, as here.

Acts ii. 28. "Thou wilt fill me (Acc.) with joy" (Gen., of joy).

Rom. xv. 13. "Now the God of hope fill you (Acc.) with all joy (Gen.) and peace (Gen.) by believing" (ἐν, *en*, with Dative). Here we have all three cases, clearly distinguished.

Rom. xv. 14. "Filled with all knowledge" (Gen., of all knowledge).

Luke ii. 40. "Filled with wisdom" (Gen., of wisdom).

2 Tim. i. 4. "Filled with joy" (Gen., of joy).

Phil. iv. 19. "My God will fill up all your need" (Acc.)

Acts ii. 2. "It filled the whole house (Acc.) where they were sitting."

Acts ii. 4. "And they were all filled with (Gen., of) *pneuma hagion*."

Acts v. 28. "Ye have filled Jerusalem (Acc.) with your doctrine" (Gen., of your doctrine).

Acts xiii. 52. "The disciples were filled with joy (Gen., of joy), and *pneuma hagion*" (Gen., of *pneuma hagion*).

Eph. iv. 10. He "ascended up far above all heavens, that he might fill all things" (Acc.).

Acts v. 3. "Why hath Satan filled thine heart?" (Acc.).

John xvi. 6. "Sorrow hath filled your heart" (Acc.).

The Greek Old Testament usage is the same:

1 Kings vii. 14. "Filled . . . with wisdom (Gen.) and understanding" (Gen.).

2 Chron. vii. 1. "The glory of JEHOVAH filled the house" (Acc.).

Hag. ii. 7 (8). "I will fill this house (Acc.) with glory" (Gen. of glory).

Jer. xiii. 12. " Every bottle shall be filled with wine " (Gen.).

It will thus be seen that the usage is uniform.

In none of these passages do we find the *Dative* case; because, when that is used it refers to the *means* whereby the thing or person, etc., is filled: the agent or instrument which effects the filling.*

'Εν (*en*) is frequently thus used in the sense of *by*, denoting agency. *See*

Mat. ix. 34 "*through* the prince of the devils."

xvii. 21 "*by* prayer and fasting."

Lu. xxii. 49 "Shall we smite *with* the sword ?"

Gal. iii. 11 "*by* law is no man justified."

1 Thess. v. 18 "This is the will of God *by* Jesus Christ."

2 Thess. ii. 13 "*through* sanctification of the Spirit."

2 Tim. i. 13 " Faith and love which are *by* Christ Jesus."

2 Tim. ii. 10 "Salvation *by* Christ Jesus."

---

* Rom. i. 29, 2 Cor. vii. 4, and Col. iv. 12, are no exceptions. In Rom. i. 29, " being filled with (Dat. *by*) all unrighteousness, &c." These are regarded here as being the characteristics of the old nature of the natural man, by which he is moved instrumentally to do all his unrighteous acts. It is *passive*, " Being filled " from the first: not the transitive act of another agency filling them with something they did not before possess.

2 Cor. vii. 4, I have been filled by (Dative, by or *by reason of*) the encouragement [given by you], I overabound with (Dat., *by reason of*) joy in all our tribulation.

When the preposition ἐν (*en*) *in*, *with* or *by* is used, it emphasizes this instrumentality.

In Col. iv. 12, all the critical Greek Texts read πεπληροφορημένοι (*peplērophorēmenoi*) "*fully assured* by God's will."

Heb. ix. 22 "purged *with* blood."

x. 10. "*by* the which will we are sanctified."*

Jas. iii. 9 "*therewith* bless we God . . . . and *therewith* curse we men."

1 Pet. i. 2 "*through* sanctification of the Spirit."

In Eph. v. 18 (the verse under consideration), ἐν πνεύματι (*en pneumati*) must be taken exactly in the same way as in chap. ii. 22; where we read that "Ye are builded together for an habitation of God *through* (or by) the Spirit."

He is the great builder; Christ is the foundation; and we are the "living stones" of this spiritual Temple, built into it by the Holy Spirit.

If it were the *pneuma* with which we were to be filled, *pneuma* would necessarily be in the Genitive case, and the Greek would have been "filled of the Spirit. *But it is not!* It is in the Dative case (emphasized by the preposition ἐν, *en*) denoting the One who fills. So that the rendering "filled with the Spirit" is quite misleading. The capital "S" is correct, for it is the Holy Spirit who is meant. But He is *the Filler*: and it is with His gifts and graces and "power from on high" that He fills the children of God.

The special gift implied by the immediate context is that of "speaking"; which is used of "spiritual" speaking, as the outcome of the operations of the Spirit. This is its meaning in ch. vi., 18.

We must note that there is no full-stop after the word Spirit. The passage goes on at once to speak of *that with which He fills.*

In Col. iii. 16, where the same "speaking" and teaching "with Psalms and Hymns and Spiritual songs" is mentioned, it is produced by the word of

---

* *i.e.*, in the Divine "Will" and purpose the elect are already in the state of sanctification spoken of. Compare Col. ii. 10.

Christ dwelling in our hearts, richly, and with all wisdom. This is the result of the Spirit's work— glorifying Christ and His word, and working in us that spiritual gift of "wisdom," and this singing with grace *in our hearts* to the Lord.

It is out of the fulness of the heart that the mouth speaketh ; and so it is, also, when our hearts are filled by the Spirit with His spiritual gifts. "Speaking" is one of these gifts, and that gift is at once evidenced. Excess of wine makes people talk. This spiritual wine also makes those who drink of it talk and sing of Him, not with their throats, but in their "hearts."

We have seen above, under Usage No. xiv., that whenever *filling* is mentioned it is always with *pneuma hagion;* and that this is "power from on high" and consists of spiritual gifts, which are the gifts of the Holy Spirit.

Eph. 6:12 (margin), "We wrestle . . . against *wicked spirits* in heavenly places." We include this marginal rendering "spirits," although the noun "*pneuma*" is not used in the Greek. It is translated "spiritual wickedness" in the text, because it is the adjective τά πνευματικά *(ta pneumatika), the spiritual things.* What it is that is "spiritual" is not stated. Their character is given, as "evil" (πονήρος, *poneros).* The R.V. supplies "hosts," and renders it, "the spiritual *hosts* of wickedness." It might well be rendered *the spiritualities of wickedness.* The word is one of four employed here to describe our spiritual enemies, and they seem to be arranged in an *epanodos* or *chiasmos.*

    a | the principalities
     b | the authorities
     b | the world-rulers
    a | the spiritual [powers]

The fourth corresponding with (being the subordinates of) the first; and the third corresponding with (being the subordinates of) the second.

Eph. 6:17   " The sword of *the pneuma*." Here the article marks the Holy Spirit; and "the Word of God" is spoken of as His sword : *i.e.*, the sword which He has provided, and uses Himself; and which He has given to us for our use. We take it as the Genitive of Possession; (the Spirit's sword), as we do " faith's shield," which is Christ (*v.* 16).

Eph. 6:18   " Praying always with all prayer and supplication through [the] *pneuma* "; *i.e.*, through the power of the Holy Spirit. The article is latent after the preposition ἐν (*en*), so often rendered " by " or " with." (See above under Eph. v. 18, 19.) He is the source and power of all prayer.

PHILIPPIANS

Phil. 1:19   " For I know that this will turn out to [my] deliverance [from bonds] through your prayers, and the bountiful supply of *the pneuma* of Jesus Christ."

The A.V. of 1611 had " s." But current editions, with R.V. have " S."

Here *pneuma* is used of what is supplied, as being quite distinct from Him who supplied it. Jesus Christ is the supplier; and what He supplies is " power from on high;" grace, patience, strength, and all needed spiritual gifts and help to support Paul in his heavy trials in his bonds.

It is remarkable that the word, here, for "supply " is ἐπιχορηγία (*epichorēgia*); and the word is used in Eph. iv. 16; where we are told how the whole body is "continually fitted together, and compacted by every sensation of SUPPLY."* So also in Gal. iii. 5, the verb is used of ministering and supplying spiritual help required by human agency.†

Here, the needed supply of spiritual power was ministered bountifully by Christ the Head, to Paul the member of His Body, in prison, sufficient for all his need.

It was this abundant supply of spiritual grace and power which thus enabled him to allow no personal consideration to keep him from rejoicing, so long as *Christ was preached* (and this, "whether in pretence or in truth," *v.* 18): and it was the same supply of grace which enabled him to allow no personal consideration, or desire to continue in life to weigh with him so long as *Christ was magnified* (*v.* 20-23). If only Christ were preached during his life, he cared not for prison. If Christ were magnified by his death, he cared not to live.

So long as Christ's cause and the cause of the Gospel, received "gain," his own "gain" did not enter into his mind.

His "bonds" had resulted in Christ's being preached by many brethren instead of by himself alone. What "gain" might not his death result in?

What wonderful spiritual power and grace must have been ministered by Christ thus to enable Paul to put

---

* See *The Church Epistles* (p. 144), by the same Author and Publisher.

† The verb ἐπιχορηγέω (*epichorēgeō*) occurs only five times: and is rendered *minister abundantly*, 2 Pet. i. 11 ; *minister*, 2 Cor. ix. 10, Gal. iii. 5 ; *have nourishment ministered*, Phil. ii. 25 ; *add*, 2 Peter i. 5.

The noun, ἐπιχορηγία (*epichorēgia*), occurs twice, Col. ii. 19 and Eph. iv. 16.

himself entirely out of all consideration ; and to think only of the "gain" and furtherance of the cause of Christ.

It was this that caused him to rejoice at being superseded by others, and to become of "no reputation"; and not to care whether he should live or die, so long as Christ should be preached, and Christ should be magnified.

Phil. 1:27   "Stand fast in one *pneuma*." Here, *pneuma* is used of that which is spiritual and invisible, in contrast with that which is outward and corporate.

The words which follow this injunction show that it relates to *the mind*: " Stand fast in one *pneuma*, with *one soul*, striving together for the faith of the Gospel." " One *pneuma* " is therefore explained as meaning " one soul," and denotes spiritual fellowship; one object, aim, and desire animating and dominating all the members of the one spiritual Body.

This is the great subject of the Epistle to the Philippians.   In Ephesians we have the whole Body : Christ the glorious Head in heaven ; and the members of that Body on Earth.

In Philippians and Colossians we have the two parts of the Body presented separately.

In Philippians we have reproof administered for the *practical* evils which come from not holding the members.

In Colossians we have correction with regard to the doctrinal evils which come from " not holding the Head " (Col. ii. 19).

These two latter of the three Prison Epistles (Philippians and Colossians), are intended to reprove and correct the failure which comes of not knowing the truth revealed in the first (Ephesians).

In Philippians, the failure is, as we have said, *practical*.

Not holding the truth concerning the *members*, there was a want of that one *pneuma*, or one mind, which Eph. iv. 1-4 emphasises as so necessary, if the spiritual unity of the members is to be preserved. This is the great theme of the whole Epistle.

In ch. ii. 2-5, we read " Fulfil ye my joy, that ye be like-minded, having the same love, being of one accord, of one mind. Let nothing be done through strife or vainglory ; but in lowliness of mind let each esteem other better than themselves. Look not every man on his own things, but every man also on the things of others. Let this mind be in you, which was in Christ Jesus also."

Then, four examples of this " one *pneuma* " are given : showing and exhibiting the lowly mind which springs from it. First there is Christ, who looked not on His own things, but the things of others (ch. ii. 6-11). Then there is Paul's own example, willing to be poured out in death as a drink-offering on their sacrifice of service, not caring whether he lived or died, himself (ch. ii. 17, 18).

Then there is the example of Timothy, "like-minded" and caring for their state, when no one else cared ; and all sought their own things, not the things which are Jesus Christ's (ch. ii. 19-24).

Then there is the example of Epaphroditus, longing after them all, and full of heaviness, not because he had been sick, but because they had heard of his sickness. His concern was for them ; therefore they could hold him in reputation, because, like his Master, he " made himself of no reputation " (ch. ii. 25-30).

When others hold themselves " in reputation " they save us the trouble of doing so. But, when any " regard not their life" (*v*. 30), like Paul (ch. i. 20-23), to supply the lack of service on the part of others who seek their own, then such can be held in reputation.

In chap. iv. 1, 2, the Philippian saints are exhorted to

stand fast in the Lord. This is the standing fast in one *pneuma* of chap. i. 27. Euodias and Syntyche were exhorted to be of "the same mind in the Lord"; thus showing the usage of *pneuma* in ch. i. 27, which is the passage under consideration.

Phil. 2:1 " If there be any fellowship of *pneuma*"; *i.e.*, any community of *spirit* or "mind." There is no article in the Greek. This, and the whole context shows that it is not the Holy Spirit who is meant here, but oneness of mind, spiritual like-mindedness. Yet both A.V. and R.V. insert the article and use " S."

Phil. 3:3 " We are the circumcision who serve (or worship) by *pneuma Theou*."

Here all the Critical Greek Texts read θεοῦ *(theou) of God* (Genitive), instead of θεῳ *(theō)* to God (Dative, *i.e.*, render service to God).

In this case *pneuma theou* would have the same meaning as in Rom. viii. 9 (see above) ; and denote the new nature, *pneuma* from God, by which alone true service can be rendered, or true worship offered.

The R.V. reading expresses in a more precise and definite manner what the Received Text means.

The A.V. inserts the article but uses " s." The R.V. also inserts the article, and uses " S," rendering it " by the Spirit of God;" and thus interprets the expression of the Holy Spirit, instead of His gift, the new nature.

Phil. 4:23 This is the second * of the three places where *pneuma* is to be added. All the Critical Greek Texts read, with R.V., "the grace of our Lord Jesus Christ be with your *pneuma*," instead of " be with you all."

It thus agrees with Gal. vi. 18 (see above).

---

* The other two are Acts iv. 25, and Rev. xxii. 6.

COLOSSIANS

Col. 1:8 "Who declared also unto us your love in [the] *pneuma*."

Here, the article may be latent after the Preposition ἐν *(en)*, *in*, or *by*, or *through*. If so, it is grammatical, and refers to the original gift of *pneuma hagion* (Acts ii. 4). Compare Rom. v. 5, where we are told how this "love of God is shed abroad in our hearts through [the] *pneuma hagion* which is GIVEN to us."

The A.V. of 1611 bears this out by having " s." In later and current editions someone without any authority has changed this to " S." The R.V. also has " S."

Col. 2:5 "For even if in flesh I am absent, yet in *the pneuma* I am with you, joying and beholding your order, and the steadfastness (or solidness) of your faith in Christ."

The usage is that of 1 Cor. v. 3, 4 ; *pneuma* being put for what is the opposite of the flesh. As we frequently say, " I cannot be with you (referring to some coming event), but I shall be thinking of you "; *i.e.*, with you in thought and mind. There is no other way of being with anyone except in the flesh.

1 THESSALONIANS

1 Thess. 1:5 "Our Gospel came not unto you in word only, but in power also, and in (or by) *pneuma hagion*, and in much assurance . . ."

1 Thess. 1:6 "Having received the word in much affliction, with joy of *pneuma hagion*."

Here, in both these verses, it denotes " power from on high," or Divine power, producing joy in affliction.

A.V. and R.V. both use capitals and insert the article. The R.V. puts " Or *Holy Spirit* " in the margin in both verses.

1 Thess. 4:8 "God, who hath also given us his *pneuma* the holy." Here Lachmann, Tischendorf, Tregelles, W.H., and R.V. read "giveth" (διδόντα, *didonta*), instead of "gave" (δόντα, *donta*).

In spite of the fact that the articles are used here, we take them as referring back to the gift of *pneuma hagion* in Acts ii. 4; for it is this which is always "given," while the Holy Spirit is always the Giver.

Moreover the words *pneuma* and *hagion* are separated by the pronoun "His," thus breaking up the expression; which would hardly be the case if the Person were meant. Both Versions use "S."

1 Thess. 5:19 "Quench not *the pneuma*." Here the article refers to the *pneuma* or spiritual gift of prophesying mentioned in the context (the next verse). The verb translated *quench* means *to extinguish*, as a light is extinguished.* In no sense can this be spoken of as being done to the Holy Spirit. No mortal can extinguish Him. But His gifts may be quenched in others. *Pneuma* is here put, by *Metonymy* (of the cause), for the spiritual gifts of the Spirit; and we can be said to extinguish these when we forbid or prevent their exercise by others who possess them (as Joshua wished to quench this same gift of prophesying in Num. xi., 28, 29). The very next sentence confirms this: "Despise not prophesyings."† The A.V. of 1611 had "s." Current editions with R.V. have "S."

---

* See Matt. xii. 20; xxv. 8. Mark ix. 44, **46, 48.** Eph. vi. 16. Heb. xi. 34.

† ἐξουθενέω (*exoutheneō*), *to set at nought*. Luke xxiii. 11, Aets iv. 11, Rom. xiv. 10, where it is so rendered; and Luke xviii. 9, Rom. xiv. 3, 1 Cor. i. 28, xvi. 11, Gal. iv. 14, where it is rendered *despise*; and 1 Cor. vi. 4, *least esteemed*; 2 Cor. x. 10, *contemptible*.

1 Thess. 5:23   "[I pray God] your *pneuma*, and soul and body may be preserved [alive] blameless, as one whole, AT (so R.V.) the coming (or *Parousia*) of our Lord Jesus Christ."

Both the A.V. and R.V. have " s," and thus agree that *pneuma* is used psychologically.

The meaning and usage of *pneuma*, and indeed, all the words in this passage must be determined by its scope. The scope of the whole context is the hope that the spirit and body should not be separated by death, but should be preserved together entire till (or at) the coming of our Lord Jesus Christ.   Verse 23 expresses the hope of ch. iv. 17, that they might be among those who should be "alive and remain" to that Coming.   The emphasis is on ὁλόκληρον (*holoklēron*), *all the parts complete, no part wanting ;* hence *entire, whole, complete* (Jas. i. 4).

The hope is that they might not die ; because, at death, the body returns to dust, and the *pneuma* to God,* and thus are separated, so that the whole man is no longer complete and entire as a " living soul."

The revelation in chap. iv. governs the whole of this fifth chapter; and this 23rd verse must be read in its light.

Indeed, the verse is made up of six lines, in which the subjects are thus set forth.

A | The work of the " God of peace."   Sanctification: complete.   (Positive).
  B | a | The *whole* person (ὁλόκληρον).
      b | One *part* of it (the *pneuma*).
  B | a | The *whole* person (the living *soul*).
      b | The other *part* of it (the body).
A | The Coming of the Lord Jesus Christ.   **Preserva**tion: without blemish.   (Negative).

---

* See Gen. iii. 19.   Job xxxiv. 15.   Psalm civ. 29.   Ecc. iii. 20; xii. 7, &c.

In the central members the truth is stated psychologically. The whole person, the living soul, is seen to consist of two parts: the *pneuma* and the *body*. The whole (a) corresponds with the whole (*a*), and the part (b) with the part (*b*). The positive (complete in all respects) is joined with "sanctify," and marks the initial stage (A). The negative (without blame) is joined with "preserved," and marks the final stage (*A*).

This will be more clearly seen if we set out the verse in full, according to the above structure, and in our own translation:

A | "Now may the God of peace Himself sanctify you completely (in all respects);

    B | a | and may your entire person (complete in all its parts),

         b | your pneuma,

    B | *a* | even your [living] soul,

         b | and your body,

  A | be preserved [alive] without blame,* at the coming of our Lord Jesus Christ."

The very title used of God, here, points us to the true scope of the passage. It is "the God of peace." Why "the God of peace"? Why not "the God of patience"? (Rom. xv. 5). Why not "the God of hope" (Rom. xv. 13)? Why "the God of peace"? Because, "peace" is peculiarly associated with resurrection. It is the first word uttered by the risen Lord. Hence, in Heb. xiii. 20, it is "the God of peace, that brought again from the dead our Lord Jesus."

So here, if we are to be preserved entire, complete in all our parts, we must be either among those who will be "alive and remain" to that coming, or among those who will be "brought again from the dead," (as

---

* "*Kept faultlessly; a complete whole.*" Only here and ch. ii. 10.

the Lord Jesus was), at His coming. Hence it is "the God of peace" to whom the prayer is made. He it is who will sanctify us, and can preserve us entire, without blame, and present us without spot to Himself in that day: for, if alive and remaining, we shall be changed; and, if brought again from the dead, we shall be raised like Him, with bodies like His own glorious body, and must therefore be, then, holy and without blame before Him in that day, and for ever.

This Scripture is written not for the purpose of giving psychological instruction, but the Apostle is writing to those for whom he prays, and he is praying for those to whom he writes. They were *alive*, when he thus wrote to them, and his prayer was that they may continue to be preserved alive, and in life, until the coming of the Lord, so that they might be then presented unto the Lord entire, as living souls.

The word "preserve" (τηρέω, *tēreō*) means *to keep, maintain* or *continue a thing in its present state*, not in some future state: and he prays that they may be preserved in life, not preserved after death. If he were praying that (whether dead or alive) they might be found blameless at the coming of Christ, then the request for the preservation of the entire person has no place; for *that* sort of preservation is assured to all "the dead in Christ." The Apostle was not praying that they might *be* blameless at that coming; but that they might be preserved alive until that coming, and thus have their part with those who shall be "alive and remain," and be thus presented blameless.

To suppose that he is praying that after death the body may be preserved in one place, and the spirit in another, renders the words "whole" and "entire" quite superfluous, and perfectly meaningless.

2 THESSALONIANS

2 Thess. 2:2   " Be not . . . troubled . . . by a *pneuma* . . . as from us."

Do not be troubled by any communication from a spirit (1 Tim. iv. 1, 2), or by any spirit-communication purporting to have come from us.

Here, *pneuma* is put by *Metonymy* (of the cause), for *the work of a spirit.*

Both Versions have " s."

The Apostle here refers to the fact that some false communication had been made to them by the agency of an evil or false brother, purporting to have come from him, to the effect that "the Day of the Lord" (R.V.) had already set in.   If it had, then Paul had deceived them ; for he had told them that that day could not overtake them as a thief (1 Thess. v. 1).   This misrepresentation had marred their hope ; for the word " hope " is omitted in 2 Thess. i. 3 (compare 1 Thess. i. 3).   Hence, he writes to tell them that that day ("the Day of the Lord") could not come till the man of sin should be revealed. The coming of that day depended on "times and seasons."   Their "gathering together unto Him" in the air did not (1 Thess. v. 1).   He writes in the interest of that blessed hope, " We beseech you *by* (ὑπέρ, *huper*, R.V. *touching*).   In all this, Paul differs from modern teachers.   They say that day cannot come till the world's conversion comes: Paul said that it could not come till the Apostacy had come, and "the man of sin" had been revealed.   They say the world is not good enough : Paul said the world is not bad enough.   But this verse shows that such teaching is the work of evil spirits and false teachers to mar or destroy the hope of our being alive and remaining till the Lord's Descension into the air to catch us up to be with Himself *before the day of the Lord* shall burst forth upon an ungodly world.

Hence this warning to these Thessalonian saints, and to ourselves.

2 Thess. 2:8   "Whom the Lord shall destroy by *the pneuma* of his mouth."

Here it is a Hebrew *idiom* for the blast of Jehovah, as explained in Isa. xi. 4.   Hos. vi. 5.   Rev. xix. 15, 21.

The A.V. has "s."   The R.V. translates it "breath"; and adds "Jesus" after "Lord" with all the Critical Greek Texts.

2 Thess. 2:13   " God hath from the beginning chosen you to salvation through sanctification of [the] *pneuma* and belief of the truth."

The article, being latent after the preposition, refers to the Holy Spirit as the Sanctifier, as in 1 Pet. i. 2; where we have the same expression, and *pneuma* is clearly one of the three Persons of the Trinity (see below).

The preposition ἐν (*en*), with the Dative, is rightly rendered "through," as it should be in Eph. v. 18.   (See p. 159).

1 TIMOTHY

1 Tim. 3:16   "Justified in *pneuma*."   Here, *pneuma* stands in contrast with "flesh" (manifested in [the] flesh).   The "flesh" refers to Incarnation.   "Seen of angels" refers to Ascension.   Therefore "justified in [the] *pneuma*" (which comes between) must refer to Resurrection, for Resurrection comes between Incarnation and Ascension.   "He was delivered [to death] on account of our offences, and was raised again on account of our justification" (Rom. iv. 25).

Pneuma, here, refers to Christ's resurrection body (see under 1 Cor. xv. 45 above).

The A.V. has "S"; though, strange to say, the R.V. has "s."

1 Tim. 4:1 (twice). "Now *the pneuma* speaketh expressly, that in the latter times some shall depart from the faith, giving heed to deceiving *pneumata* and teachings of demons."

In this verse *pneuma* occurs twice, and is used in two distinct senses. The first refers to the Holy Spirit; and the latter to evil angels, as distinct from "demons."

Both Versions are correct, therefore, in using "S" with the first; and "s" with the second.

1 Tim. 4:12 "In *pneuma*." All the Critical Greek Texts agree in omitting these words with R.V.

This is the seventh omission which we have to note.*

2 TIMOTHY

2 Tim. 1:7 "God hath not given us a *pneuma* of cowardice," *i.e.*, a cowardly spirit. The word being used here in the sense of character (see above: Usage, No. VII., page 20). Both Versions use "s."

2 Tim. 1:14 "That good deposit † (see R.V. margin) guard by [the] *pneuma hagion* that dwelleth in us." This deposit was the wondrous Secret or "Mystery" received by *pneuma hagion*, and specially committed in the first instance to the Apostle Paul. In 1 Tim. i. 11 he calls it "the gospel of the glory of the blessed God which I, even I, was entrusted with."

In 2 Tim. i. 12 he declares his faith that God "is able to keep guard over my deposit (παραθήκην, *parathēkēn*), mine because He has committed to me, with a view to that day." There is nothing about "I have committed unto

---

* The other passages being Luke ii. 40; ix. 35. Acts xviii. 5. Rom. viii. 1. 1 Cor. vi. 20. Eph. v. 9. 1 Peter i. 22. 1 John v. 7.

† All the Critical Greek Texts (with R.V.) read παραθήκην (*parathēkēn*) *deposit*, instead of παρακαταθήκην (*parakatathēkēn*).

Him " in the Greek. The R.V. margin says, "*that
which he hath committed unto me*. Greek, *my deposit*."

Those who had heard Paul had turned away from him
and his teaching, as he tells Timothy in verse 15, "All
they which are in Asia be turned away from me." Those
very persons, who for two whole years had heard more
about it than any others (see Acts xix. 10), had given it up.
But he says in verse 12, " I know whom I have believed ;
and am persuaded that He is able to take care of that
precious deposit that He hath committed unto me.
And now, Timothy—do you, in your turn, guard it."
He thus solemnly exhorts him,

" O Timothy, guard the deposit * committed unto thee,
turning away from the profane babblings and oppositions
of the knowledge which is falsely so called ; which some,
professing, have erred concerning THE faith."

Then again in 2 Tim. i. 14 (the verse we are considering) there is the same exhortation to guard this deposit,
the revelation of the Mystery or Secret concerning
"Christ and the church."

These are the only three places where the noun
παραθήκη *(parathēkē), deposit*, occurs. (1 Tim. vi. 20
and 2 Tim. i. 14, in the Critical Texts; and 2 Tim. i. 12,
according to these and the Received Text as well). The
very confusion in the Greek Text over the passages
which have to do with the Mystery† is a sad proof of

---

* All the Critical Greek Texts read this precisely as they do
in 2 Tim. i. 14, as noted above. And the R.V. puts in the
margin " Greek, *the deposit*."

† See these three passages : also 1 Cor. ii. 1, and 1 Tim. iii. 16.
Transcribers, *not understanding* what they were copying from
the more ancient Manuscripts, would naturally be tempted to
make it conform to what they did believe and understand.

In 1 Tim. iii. 16, " God manifest in the flesh," the word rendered "God " was in all probability originally written Ὅ (*ho*),
which.

the fact that it was given up in the Apostle Paul's own life-time (as is stated in 2 Tim. i. 15).

It is a fact that most of even the ancient MSS. exhibit a correction at this place ; and, as the truth of the Mystery was so soon forsaken, it is not to be wondered at that ῟Ο (*ho*), *which*, could not be understood. ῟Ο (*ho*) is the neuter gender, and it agreed with Μυστήριον (*mustērion*), *Mystery*, to which it refers. But, the *Mystery* being forgotten, it was altered by some scribe into "ΟC " (*hos*), *who: i.e.*, from the neuter into the masculine.

῟Ο (*ho*), *which*, is a reading of sufficient ancient importance to be noted in the R.V. margin. Zahn, (in his *Forschungen*, Vol. iii., Beilage iv., p. 277 quoted by Nestlé in his *Introduction to the Textual Criticism of the Greek New Test*, p. 317), published two or three lines from some parchment fragments in the Egyptian Museum of the Louvre, which he thinks belongs to the IV.-VI. Centuries, and contain this reading.

It is also the reading of D (The Cambridge MS. or Codex Bezæ, belonging to Cent. V. or VI.

It can be easily understood how, when in the midst of controversies concerning the Deity of Christ, it would be a great temptation to put a little mark in the middle of the Ο, and turn it into Θ (*th*), by which the pronoun ΟC would then become ΘC, the abbreviated form for Θεός (*theos*), *God*. This is the contested reading of the Alexandrine MS. in the British Museum (some declaring that it is a mark that shows through from the other side of the leaf—a statement, the truth of which, the use of microscopes has been enabled to establish). It is a fact that the Sinaitic MS. reads ΟC, *who*, but a fourth hand has corrected it to ΘC. It may also be stated that in the MS., D which gives ῟Ο (*ho*), *which* as the original reading of the MS., a third hand has altered it again to ΟC (*who*).

Hence the R.V. says in the margin,

"The word *God*, in place of *He who*, rests on no sufficient ancient evidence. Some ancient authorities read *which*."

And, judging by the internal evidence of the Epistles to Timothy, we agree with this latter reading.

In 1 Cor. ii. 1, The Alexandrine (Cent. IV.), Ephræmi (Cent. V.), and Sinaitic (Cent. IV.), and all the Critical Greek Texts agree in reading " *Mystery*" instead of " *Testimony*." Tregelles does not even concede it a place in his margin.

The revelation of the "Mystery" was by *pneuma hagion*, or "power from on high." It was "the deposit" entrusted to Paul, and by him to Timothy and others, who were solemnly charged to guard it with all care.

Both Versions insert the Article and use Capitals. The R.V. says, in the margin, " Or, *Holy Spirit*."

2 Tim. 4:22   "The Lord be with thy *pneuma*." Here, all the Critical Greek Texts and R.V. omit "Jesus Christ." Alford puts it in brackets. " Thy *pneuma* " is put here, by *Synecdoche*, for thyself; *i.e.*, with thee. Both A.V. and R.V. have " s."

TITUS

Titus 3:5   " Not as the result of works of right-eousness which we ourselves did (see R.V.), but according to his mercy, he saved us through the washing (or purify-ing) of a new birth, even [the] new creation of *pneuma hagion*."

Here the work of salvation is described as having been the work of God; and it is declared to be not the work of man by his own good works, but the act of God: " HE SAVED US.'" How? Not by the washing or purifying with material water, but with the spiritual water (see above under John iii. 5), even the New creation of *pneuma hagion*.

These are the meanings of the two words: παλιγγενεσία (*palingenesia*) translated " regeneration," *new birth* — or *re-creation, new creation*; it occurs only here and Matt. xix. 28: ἀνακαίνωσις *(anakainōsis)* translated "re-newing," means *a making anew*. It occurs only here and Rom. xii. 2.

The subject of this verse is the Divine act of the new birth, by which the New nature, *pneuma hagion*, is im-parted, and the new creation is effected.

This verse has no reference to baptism with

material water by man, but the new-creation work of God in the new birth, which is a baptism with the spiritual medium of *pneuma hagion*.

The only other place where λουτρόν (*loutron*) occurs is Eph. v. 26; where, as here, it is translated "*washing*." In both places the R.V. gives "*laver*" in the margin. But note that in both these passages it is the act of God, and *He uses no laver!* In Eph. v. 26, it is again His act, "that HE might sanctify it, having cleansed it by the washing of water (not material water, but by the spiritual medium) by the Word."

So here: "HE saved us," not by material washings in material water; or by works of righteousness which we did ourselves (R.V.), but by the washing of *pneuma hagion* of the new birth, even the new creation.

PHILEMON

Phil. 25 "The grace of our Lord Jesus Christ be with your *pneuma*." Here, *pneuma* is put by *Synecdoche* for *yourself*. Both Versions have "s."

HEBREWS

Heb. 1:7 "Who maketh his angels *pneumata*"; *i.e.*, they are "made," or created, spiritual beings, and not *human* beings. See verse 14.

A human being has "flesh and blood."

A risen and changed human being has "flesh and bones" (Luke xxiv. 39). In the resurrection body *pneuma* takes the place of "blood;" and hence the resurrection body is called a "spiritual body." (See above, on 1 Cor. xv. 45).

Compare Psalm civ. 4: where the A.V. has "s;" while the R.V. translates Heb. i. 7 "winds" and puts "*spirits*" in the margin; but in Ps. civ. 4 the R.V. has *winds* both in text and margin.

Heb. 1:14 The same as verse 7 above. Both Versions have "s."

Heb. 2:4 "With divers miracles, and gifts (margin *distributions*) of *pneuma hagion*." These "spiritual gifts" were distributed, as stated here, as well as in 1 Cor. xii. 11, "according to his own will." Both Versions insert the article, and use capitals.

Heb. 3:7 "Wherefore as *the pneuma the holy* saith, To-day if ye will hear his voice."

Here, it is the Holy Spirit, as the direct Inspirer of Scripture, speaking through "holy men of God."

Heb. 4:12 "The Word of God is quick (or living) and powerful, and sharper than any two-edged sword, piercing even to the dividing asunder of both *psychē* and *pneuma*, of both joints and marrow, and able to judge* thoughts and intents of heart."

Here *psychē* (translated "soul,") is used of what is natural, and *pneuma* ("spirit") is used of what is spiritual; what is of man as a natural human being, and what is of God; what is human, and what is Divine; what is of the flesh, and what is of the *pneuma*, according to John iii. 6.

"The Word of God": *i.e.*, the living Word (the Lord Jesus Christ), and the written Word (the Scriptures of truth), are able, and are appointed, to be the judges of men (John v. 22, 27, and xii. 48). And they are "able to judge" and condemn the "thoughts and intents of the heart": *i.e.*, the Old nature. Both Versions have "s."

Heb. 6:4-6 "For it is impossible for those who were . . . partakers of *pneuma hagion* . . . if they shall fall away, to renew them again unto repentance."

Here, though there is no article in the Greek, both

---

*Greek, κριτικός *(kritikos) able to judge, skilled in judging*: hence, our Eng. "Critic." But it is the Word of God that is the critic or judge of man: and not man, who dares to arrogate to himself the right to judge the Word of God.

Versions interpolate it in the English, and use Capital letters, of the Holy Spirit. But the passage speaks of those who had " gifts." Nothing is said about their having received " grace." It is possible to have the one without the other. A man may have *grace*, but no " gifts": and another may have *gifts*, but no " grace." Balaam had gifts, but not grace. He had the gift of prophecy from the Lord (Num. xxiii. 5, 16), but he was " none of His." For it is " grace that saves," and not " gifts " (Eph. ii. 8). Grace is the great " gift," without which all others are of no avail.

Judas, as one of the Twelve, doubtless shared their miraculous gifts, which were given to all of them (see Matt. x. 1).

The Lord Himself tells us of those who will have done " many wonderful works," but who will be rejected because they had not *grace* (see Matt. vii. 21-23).

This is also the teaching of 1 Cor. xiii. 1-3.

It is now as it was in the Old Testament Dispensation : *pneuma* may " come upon " persons for *service*, without being " within " them for *salvation*.

These Hebrews were believers ; but many of them believed no more than those Jews in Acts xxi. 20, of whom there were " many thousands who believed," but were " all zealous of the Law." We are not told what they believed ; or how much they believed. Whether, as Jews, they believed in Christ as the Messiah of Israel ; or whether, as lost sinners, they believed in Christ as the Saviour. They could hardly have taken the place of sinners, or be on the ground of *grace*, if they were still " zealous of the Law."

Hence, these words in Heb. vi. may well have been addressed to such Hebrew believers as they were : but they have no application to-day to those whose standing is in grace, according to Rom. viii., Eph. ii., &c., and who are members of the Body of Christ, *in Whom* there is "no condemnation" and *from Whom* there is no separation.

The whole passage speaks of "gifts." They had "tasted" the "powers of the world to come." They had had a foretaste of millennial days in those early (transitional) chapters of the Acts. But the unbelieving Jews rejected Christ as the Messiah; and many who believed He was the Messiah rejected Him as the Saviour: rejecting His sacrifice by going back to the sacrifices of the Law (Acts xxi. 20., Gal. iv. 9).

All such were warned that "there remaineth no more sacrifice for sins" (Heb. x. 26); and that without a sacrifice they were without hope, and must be lost.

Heb. 9:8 "*The pneuma the holy*, this signifying." Here the statement is that the Holy Spirit, in inspiring Moses to write the account of the Tabernacle in Exodus, had a meaning beyond what Moses himself understood. It does not say that Moses "signified" anything in what he wrote; but the Holy Spirit "signified" many deep spiritual truths, which He revealed to the Apostle Paul, and afterwards made known to us, through him, in this Epistle to the Hebrews.

Heb. 9:14 "Who through eternal *pneuma* offered Himself without spot to God."

Here, it is the Holy Spirit, although there is no article. It is there, grammatically, being latent after the preposition διά (dia) *through* or *by means of*. It was *by means of* the energy of the Holy Spirit that Christ's spotless human nature was formed (Lu. i. 35), and could be "offered to God" on our behalf.

Heb. 10:15 "Whereof *the pneuma the holy* also is a witness to us."

As in ch. ix. 8.: the Holy Spirit was the direct Inspirer of the words written in Jer. xxxi. 33, 34, which are quoted here; and therefore of all that was spoken and written by His prophets (Heb. i. 1; 2 Pet. i. 21).

Heb. 10:29 "And hath done despite unto (*i.e.*, insulted) *the pneuma* of grace."

By the rejection of Christ, the Jews had trodden under foot the Son of God, and counted the blood of the Covenant (wherewith He was sanctified) an unholy thing. They had thus insulted the Holy Spirit, the Author and Giver of all grace, by Whose power and gift the blessings and grace of this new Covenant had been brought to them.

Rejecting Christ's Sacrifice, there remained for them no other, "no more sacrifice for sins." Their own sacrifices had all been done away by His one sacrifice; and, despising that, no other sacrifice was left for them.

This must not be applied to the Members of the Body of Christ to-day. "If we sin, we have an advocate with the Father" (I John ii. 1, 2). But the sin of those Hebrews who are here specially referred to, is quite another matter altogether.

Heb. 12:9 "Shall we not much rather be in subjection unto the Father of the *pneumata* (*i.e.*, our *pneumata*), and live?"

The A.V. of 1611 had "S": but the current editions, and R.V., have "s." The latter, in the margin, suggests "*our spirits.*"

The point is that our earthly parents (the authors of our bodies) discipline these bodies, which die. Shall we not much rather be in subjection to our heavenly Father, who is the Author and Giver of our spirits? The profit of their discipline was only for "a few days;"

but the profit of His discipline is for ever and ever.
" We shall live," means, *live again* in resurrection.*

Heb. 12:22,23   " Ye are come . . . to God the Judge
of all, and to [the] *pneumata* of [the] just [who]
have been perfected " [in resurrection].

The future heavenly sphere of blessing in Christ, to
which these Hebrews " came " under the New Covenant,
is here contrasted with the earthly sphere of blessing,
into which they came under the old Covenant by Moses.
That was " sight."   The New is " faith."

Those Hebrews who now believed were partakers of a
New Covenant, in which all is spiritual, real, Divine and
heavenly : *but all is future ;* as is clear from verses 26-28,
that follow.   In the past, the Old Covenant was material,
and repellent : In the New Covenant all is Spiritual,
though real; and Heavenly, not earthly ; and future, not
present or past.

" God, the judge of all," tells of future judgment :
the next clause therefore must refer to resurrection,
without which their will be no judgment.   Hence, the
resurrection of the wicked dead is called " [the] resurrection of judgment " (John v. 27-29).   The just will be
perfected only by resurrection.   Even now, we are
imperfect; and Death leaves us still more imperfect :
" unclothed," with body and spirit separated.   The body
(at death) returns " to the earth as it was, and the *pneuma*
returns to God, who gave it " (Ecc. xii. 7).   Both are
imperfect till resurrection.   Then they will be united
in glory, and thus the just will be " made perfect."

---

* This is the meaning of ζάω (*zaō*) very frequently.   See
Matt. ix. 18.   Mark xvi. 11.   Luke xxiv. 5, 23.   John. xi. 25, 26.
Acts i. 3 ; ix. 41 ; xxv. 19.   Rom. vi. 10 ; xiv. 9 (so all the
Critical Greek Texts).   2 Cor. xiii. 4.   Rev. i. 18 ; ii. 8; xiii. 14 ;
xx. 4, 5 (so all the Critical Greek Texts).   See *Things to Come*,
Vol. VIII., page 142.

Till then, till the coming of the Lord and the resurrection of His People, all is imperfect; all is incomplete.

The Apostle Paul, in writing to the Thessalonian Saints, tells them how he longed to see once again the grace bestowed upon and manifested by them. He prayed that God might direct his way to them. Satan might hinder such fellowship here (1 Th. ii. 17, 18). Distance might divide them. Death might separate them. There was no hope, no joy, no crown of rejoicing, until they, and he, should find it "in the presence of our Lord Jesus Christ at his coming" (1 Thess. ii. 19. Compare Chap. iii. 9-13).

In writing to the Corinthian saints he tells them how he would rather not be "unclothed" in death (2 Cor. v. 4), but "clothed upon" with "the building of God," the "house (or body) not made with hands," and that thus "mortality might be swallowed up of life" (not death) ! (*vv.* 1-4).

Heb. xii. 23 stands in direct relation to Heb. xi. 40. The "elders," who lived by faith, and had the promises made to them personally (" to THEE and to thy seed "),* all "died in faith," and "did not receive the promises." They *will* receive them in resurrection; but they will not be "made perfect" in resurrection, apart from (χωρίς, *choris*) us. That is to say, those who had "died in faith" will not rise before "us" (*i.e.*, their fellow Hebrew believers), but will with them have part in "the first resurrection" (Rev. xx. 5, 6). All of them will be raised according to 1 Cor. xv. 23. They in their own rank or order will have part in the "first resurrection," and will thus be "made perfect," before the thousand years. "The rest of the dead"

*See *Things to Come* for August, 1903.

will not be raised till after the thousand years
(Rev. xx. 1-6).*

JAMES

Jas. 2:26 " The body without *pneuma* is dead, just
as faith also† without works is dead."

The use of *pneuma* here is psychological, according to
Gen. ii. 7, Ps. civ. 29, Ecc. xii. 7, &c. The A.V. puts
" *breath* " in the margin. Both A.V. and R.V., insert
the article, but put " s."

The true *application* of this statement depends on the
truth—true interpretation—of the fact stated.

It illustrates the previous passage. " As the body
without *pneuma* is dead," so the personal organism (the
" living soul"), the man, is imperfect till resurrection.

It illustrates 2 Cor. iii. 6, 17. " As the body without
pneuma is dead," so the Old Covenant also without
Christ (its *pneuma*) is dead: and the letter of the Old
Testament, yea, the whole Word of God also, is dead,
without Christ, who is its *pneuma*. As it is said of the
New Jerusalem " the Lamb is the light thereof"; so
may it be said of the Word of God—Christ is the life,
or the *pneuma*, thereof. (See under 2 Cor. iii. 6).

---

*All this is, of course, quite apart from the raising of those
who, being members of " the body of Christ," have fallen asleep.
These will rise at the coming forth of the Lord into the air and
be changed and caught up to meet Him there, and be for ever
with Him. The " first " resurrection in Rev. xx. is the *former
of the two there mentioned*, and will not take place till after the
destruction of the Beast and the false prophet, and the binding
of Satan. Not the first resurrection since the world began, but
the first (or former) of the two which had been the subject of
revelation, and are the subject of Rev. xx. 1-6. The Resurrection
spoken of in 1 Thess. iv. is the subject of a special revelation " by
the Word of the Lord," and had not been made known to the
sons of men till that moment.

† The word " also " goes with the word " faith," not " dead."

Jas. 4:5,6   " Do ye think that the Scripture saith in vain *the pneuma* within us lusteth to envy ?   But he giveth a greater grace " (so R.V. margin).

Here *pneuma* is used psychologically, of the invisible motions of the mind, which are called *pneuma*, by *Metonymy* ; in contrast with the body which is visible.

These motions are always evil, and evil continually, *as the Scripture saith* (see Gen. vi. 5; viii. 21, &c.)   This is the statement of the previous verse (*v.* 4), which is here being established by the reference to the universal testimony of scripture as to the Old nature, or the natural man. (See 1 Cor. ii. 14. Rom. vii. 18; viii. 5, 7. John iii. 6.   Matt. xv. 13, &c., &c.)

The next verse tells us that, though this be so, though by nature our will is " enmity against God " (Rom. viii. 7), yet God gives a New nature, which is here called " a greater grace " (so the Greek, see R.V. margin).   It was grace in the old creation (Gen. ii. 7); but, since man is fallen, the gift of the New nature is truly " a greater grace."   Both Versions use " s."

1 PETER

1 Peter 1:2   " Through sanctification by [the] *pneuma*."

The article is latent after the preposition, and is as clearly implied before *pneuma*, as it is before the words "foreknowledge," " father," and " obedience " in the same verse.   It means, therefore, the Holy Spirit.

1 Peter 1:11   " Searching what, or what manner of time *the pneuma* in them did signify concerning Christ."

The use of the article here, distinguishes *the pneuma Christou* from a similar expression in Rom. viii. 9 (where it is without the article), and is used of the New nature. Here, the words " in them " are inserted (in the Greek) between " the " and " pneuma."   Emphasizing the action of the Holy Spirit* in inspiring them with prophecies concerning Christ's "sufferings" and "glories." We take the Genitive to be that of *Relation:* for it was concerning Christ, that the Holy Spirit communicated those prophecies to the prophets.

The prophets did not understand "what *time*" was signified in this revelation: whether the glory was to follow immediately on the sufferings, or whether there was to be an interval between them; and, if so, how long it was to be. Hence "they searched, and searched diligently," to see "what, or *what manner of time* the Spirit-in-them signified concerning Christ, when it testified beforehand as to the sufferings of Christ, and the glory that should follow."

The prophets told of both: but, though they often foretold and testified concerning the glory without referring to the sufferings, they never testified of the sufferings without telling of the glory of which they were the foundation. (See Ps. xxii., Is. liii., &c.: and compare Matt. xvi. 21 and 27, Luke xxiv. 26, 1 Pet. iv. 13, v. 1 and 10, 11).

1 Peter 1:12 They "preached the gospel unto you with *pneuma hagion* sent down from heaven."

They preached with "power from high," sent down in Acts ii. 4. See under Acts i. 5, ii. 4, &c.

Both versions insert the article, and use capital letters. The R.V. puts "*Holy Spirit*" in the margin.

1 Peter 1:22 "Seeing ye have purified your souls [*i.e.*, yourselves] in your obedience to the truth through [the] *pneuma*."

This is the eighth place where the word *pneuma* is to be omitted, for all the Critical Greek Texts with R.V. omit διὰ πνεύματος (*dia pneumatos*), *through [the] spirit.*

---

* Both versions have " S " correctly.

1 Peter 3:4   "The ornament of a meek and quiet *pneuma*." Here *pneuma* is put by Metonymy (of the cause) for the demeanour and character produced by the New nature. It is thus used of character. (See under usage No. vii., page 20). Both versions put "s."

1 Peter 3:18   "Having been put to death indeed (μέν, *men*, which neither A.V. nor R.V. translates) as to the flesh, but made alive* as to the *pneuma*."†

The A.V. has "S" whereas the R.V. has "s."

Resurrection is here meant. It is in 1 Cor. xv. 44-46 that *pneuma* is used of Christ's risen body. (See also Luke xxiv. 39, above).

The *pneuma* as part of man (psychologically) is alive in itself, and can never die, though the body sees corruption : the *pneuma* "returns to God who gave it." The *pneuma*, therefore, needs not to be, and cannot be, "made alive." It is man, the "living soul," who is "made alive" in resurrection, and is thereby and then made a *pneuma* or spiritual being (1 Cor. xv. 46).

So Christ, though He was put to death, as to the flesh, was raised a spiritual body.

1 Peter 3:19   " By (or in) which [resurrection body] to the-in-prison-*pneumata* also, he went and made proclamation

(disobedient as they once were (Gen. vi.) when the longsuffering of God was waiting in Noah's days, while an ark was preparing, into which [hav-

---

*ζωοποιέω (*zōopoieō*) *to make alive in resurrection.* See John v. 21, Rom. iv. 17, viii. 11, 1 Cor. xv. 22, 36, and note on page 182.

† All the Critical Greek Texts omit the article before *pneuma*. The Revisers omit it in their Greek Text but not in their English translation. The Dative case here, both of " flesh " and " spirit," is the Dative of reference.

ing gone], a few, that is eight souls (*i.e.*, persons) were brought safely through * water; which [water], the antitype [of that], now saves you also,† [even] baptism :—not the putting away of [the] filth of [the] flesh (*i.e.*, fleshly filth) [with water], but [the] answer of a good conscience toward God, by [the] resurrection of Jesus Christ).

—who is at the right hand of God, having gone into heaven, angels, and authorities, and powers having been made subject to Him."

Here the word "*spirits*" refers to angels. Man is never called or spoken of as *a pneuma*. In all these 385 passages not one can be found where man, in any condition (past, present or future), is called "a spirit": not one: for a spirit "hath not flesh and bones." Angels are so called, but not man. In resurrection, man will be raised with "a spiritual body" (2 Cor. v. 2‡) like that with which the Lord Jesus rose (Phil. iii. 21). These angels "once were disobedient;" and this disobedience, here, is set in contrast with the obedience of those "angels" spoken of in verse 22 as being "subject" and therefore obedient to Christ.

Angels are called in the Old Testament "sons of God." In every place where this expression occurs,§ it means angels: *i.e.*: angelic or spiritual beings. No one can give us authority to take the words in Gen. vi. 1, in a

*The Greek here, διασώζειν *(diasōzein)*, is always used of *bodily saving*, in all its eight occurrences :—Matt. xiv. 36. Luke vii. 3. Acts xxiii. 24 ; xxvii. 43, 44 ; xxviii. 1, 4 ; and 1 Peter iii. 20. It thus differs from the simple σώζειν *(sozein)*, *to save*, in the next verse.

† So all the Critical Greek Texts.

‡ The word οἰκητήριον *(oikētērion)* is used of a *spiritual body* only in 2 Cor. v. 2 and Jude 6.

§ Gen. vi. 2, 4 ; Job. i. 6 ; ii. 1 ; xxxviii. 7 ; Ps. xxix. 1 ; lxxxix. 6 ; Dan. iii. 25 (Hos. i. 10 is a different expression altogether).

different sense from that which they have in every other place, in the Old Testament.

The "fall of the angels" is a historical fact: and spoken of as distinctly, though not described so fully as is "the fall of man."

In Jude 6 we are told that "they kept not their first estate, but left* their own habitation."† What this means, or what it involves, we cannot tell; and no one can tell us. Whatever it was it made their sin possible; which, otherwise, with our present knowledge, seems to us impossible.‡

That it was thus possible for them to sin as recorded in Gen. vi. 1-4 is clearly implied in Jude 7, where their sin is compared to the sin of "Sodom and Gomorrha, and the cities about them IN LIKE MANNER, giving themselves over to fornication, and going after strange§ flesh, are set forth as an example suffering the vengeance of eternal fire."

Gen. vi. 1-4 further describes their sin, and tells us that their progeny was called *nephīlīm* or *fallen ones*.‖ So awful was this progeny, and so monstrous in every sense of the word, that it doubtless became the basis of the heathen mythology. That mythology did not have its origin in the imagination of man, but it had its historical basis in fact; and that fact the Scripture thus explains to us.

So terrible were the results of this fall of the angels,

---

* ἀπολείπω (*apoleipō*) *to leave completely*, or, *leave behind*. Compare 2 Tim. iv. 13, 20.

† οἰκητήριον (*oikētērion*) used only here and 2 Cor. v. 2 of *a spirit-body*.

‡ In Luke viii. 29 a *pneuma* could tear and rend a man.

§ ἕτερος (*heteros*) *different*, of another kind: not ἄλλος (*allos*), *another* of the same kind.

‖ נְפִלִים (*nephīlīm*) *fallen ones*, from נָפַל (*nāphal*) *to fall*.

that no judgment short of the Flood would serve to destroy them all.

So universal was it, that only one family was found untainted. Of Noah, it says, "These are the generations (*i.e.*, the family pedigree) of Noah: Noah was a just man, and perfect (*i.e.*, without blemish)* in (or among) his generations"† (*i.e.*, among his contemporaries), Gen. vi. 9. Hence, all mankind had to be destroyed, except the family of Noah.

There was another irruption of fallen angels "AFTER THAT." This is expressly stated in Gen. vi. 4, as being *after the Flood.* Their progeny was called נְפִילִים (*nephīlim*) *fallen ones.* See Gen. vi. 4. They are so called also in Numbers xiii. 33, where the word is again rendered "giants:" and they were known as "sons of Anak" (from a prominent Canaanite in Moses's day, Anak is spoken of as of the *Nephīlīm*). They were also known as *Rephaīm*, רְפָאִים, after another prominent character named *Rapha*: hence they were called *sons of Rapha*, or *Rephaīm.* See Deut. ii. 11, 20, which shows they were also known as *Emim* by the Moabites. Compare Deut. iii. 11, 13. Josh. xii. 4; xiii. 12; xv. 8; xvii. 15; xviii. 16. 1 Ch. xx. 4, 6, 8.

This second irruption was evidently not so extensive as the first; though they were numerous enough to populate the land of Canaan, but could be dealt with and destroyed with the Sword, and did not necessitate another Flood.

---

* תָּמִים (*tāmīm*) means *without physical defect.* It is the word used of sacrifices, &c., being *without blemish.*

† This is a different word from that rendered "generations" in the former part of the verse. The former word is תּוֹלְדוֹת (*tōl'dōth*) *family pedigree.* The latter word is דּוֹר (*dōr*), *contemporaries.*

It was the special mission of Israel to destroy this corrupt race of Canaanitish nations. This extermination was imperative, as was the judgment of the Flood. And yet there are those so-called " philanthropists " who can speak of the " cruelty " of God in using Israel to destroy these nations. Infidels never tire of charging God with cruelty ; not knowing the awful ancestry, or the nature and character, of this corrupt race. The judgment executed by Israel was a mercy (Ps. cxxxvi. 20) to the whole human race.

It was the sight of these horrible creatures that so frightened the twelve spies (Num. xiii. 28-33). And it was the first great victory over them that makes the destruction of " Og, King of Bashan," so celebrated in Israel's history. (Num. xxi ; Read Josh. xii. xiii. ; xv. 8. ; xvii. 15 ; xviii. 16 ; Ps. cxxxvi. 20.) David completed the work of destruction. (1 Chron. xx. 4, 6, 8. Compare 2 Sam. xxi. 16, 18, 20, 22).

As to the angels themselves, as they were spirit-beings they could not be thus destroyed, like their monstrous progeny ; but they were put " in prison " (1 Pet. iii. 19) and are " kept in chains," and " in darkness, reserved unto judgment (to come)." See 2 Pet. ii. 4 ; where they are mentioned in connection with Noah (*v.* 5) as they are also in 1 Pet. iii. 20.

The context of 1 Pet. iii. 18-22 shows that the passage is the continuation of what precedes, as it commences with the word " For."

The scope of the passage shows that those to whom Peter was inspired to write, were suffering great and heavy trials,* and needed encouragement to enable them to endure their suffering for well-doing. Verse 17 (of ch. iii.) tells them that " it is better, if the will of God be so, that ye suffer for well doing than for evil doing."

---

*See 1 Pet. i. 7 ; ii. 20-23 ; iii. 14-17 ; iv. 12-19.

Then the argument goes on :
FOR Christ also suffered.   He was even put to death as
to His flesh ; and that was for well doing, indeed.

But He was raised again from the dead ; and thus had
a glorious triumph.   And His triumph was so great that
He went and proclaimed* His victory, so that it
reached even to the imprisoned spirits.†   Then, ye may
well suffer ; for ye suffer for " well doing," and ye
shall have a like glorious triumph.   Ye may " suffer "
now ; but " the glory " will surely follow, in your case,
(ch. iv. 13) as it did in His.

This is the scope of the passage—and no other explanation of " the-in-prison-spirits " will satisfy the whole
context, of which this verse is only a part; being introduced by the word " for," which connects it indissolubly
with what precedes.

1 Peter 4:6   This verse is also introduced as a
reason for what is said in verse 5 ; and it must be
interpreted in harmony with the context.

The argument is, that those who did them evil " shall
give account to Him that is ready to judge the quick
(*i.e.*, the living) and the dead.   FOR to this end was
the Gospel preached to those [now] dead also,‡ that

---

*The word is *not* εὐαγγελίζω *(euangelizō) to preach the Gospel ;*
but it is κηρύσσω *(kērussō) to make proclamation as a herald* (from
κῆρυξ, *kērux, a herald*).   It does not mean *to preach* in any sense
of the word, but *to herald* that which is determined or defined by
the context.

† In 2 Pet. ii. 4 this prison is τάρταρος *(Tartaros)* not
Hades, or *Gekenna.*   Not "hell " as in A.V. and R.V.   The noun
τάρταρος *(tartaros)* does not occur at all in the New Testament ;
and the verb ταρταρόω *(tartaroō)* only here : and should be
rendered : " but having cast them to the deepest abyss, delivered
them to pits of darkness to be reserved for judgment."

‡ νεκροί *(nekroi)* without the article, always means dead
people, regarded as having been once alive, but are now dead.
See Deut. xiv. 1 ; Matt. xxii. 32 ; Mark ix. 10 ; Luke xvi. 30, 31,

THOUGH* they might be judged according to [the will of] men as to the flesh, YET they might live [again] † according to [the will of] God as to *pneuma.*"‡ (*i.e.*, as to their spiritual resurrection body, 1 Cor. xv. 44, 45).

Here, therefore, *pneuma* refers to the spiritual resurrection body. Both A.V. and R.V. use " s " here.

1 Peter 4:14 " If ye are reproached in (so Greek) [the] name of Christ blessed are ye; because *the* [*pneuma*] of glory, even *the pneuma* of God resteth upon you."

The Ellipsis in the first clause is to be supplied by repeating the word *pneuma* from the second clause.

The figure is *Hendiadys*; showing that though two expressions are used : only One—the Holy Spirit—is meant. The two descriptions are synthetic ; the second expanding the first.

The interpretation of the Figure would be—"because the glorious, yea, the Divine Spirit resteth upon you." The A.V. has " s." The R.V. has " S."

---

xxiv. 46 ; Acts xxiii. 6 ; xxiv. 15 ; xxvi. 8 ; Rom. vi. 13 ; x. 7 ; xi. 15 ; Heb. xi. 19 ; xiii. 20 ; 1 Cor. xv. 12, 13, 15, 16, 20, 21, 29 (2nd word) 32.

οἱ νεκροί (*hoi nekroi*) with the article always means *dead bodies, corpses.* See Gen. xxiii. 3, 4, 6, 8, 13, 15 ; Deut. xxviii. 26 ; Jer. xii. 3 ; Ezek. xxxvii. 9 ; Matt. xxii. 31 ; Luke xxiv. 5 ; 1 Cor. xv. 29 (1st and 3rd words) 35, 42, 52.

* The work μέν (*men*) *though,* is left untranslated both in the A.V. and R.V., though they have translated the related word δέ (*de*) *but.*

† ζάω (*zaō*) means not only *to live*, but, when used in this connection (after the mention of death), it means *to live again* in resurrection, see Matt. ix. 18. Acts ix. 41. Mark xvi. 11. Luke xxiv. 5, 23. John xi. 25, 26. Acts i. 3 ; xxv. 19. Rom. vi. 10 ; xiv. 9. 2 Cor. xiii. 4. Rev. i. 18 ; ii. 8 ; xiii. 14 ; xx. 4, 5.

‡ We translate κατὰ ἀνθρώπους (*kata anthrōpous*) *according to* [the will of] *men* (or the judgment of men) : and κατὰ θεόν (*kata Theon*) according [to the will of] God, as the A.V. renders the very same words in Rom. viii. 27, putting " *the will of* " in italics as we have in brackets.

2 PETER

2 Peter 1:19-21   "And we have more sure the prophetic word, to which ye do well that ye take heed (as to a lamp shining in a dark place, until the Day dawn, and the Morning Star arise), in your hearts;* knowing this first, that any prophecy of Scripture never came† of its own‡ unfolding§ (or sending forth): for not by the will of man was prophecy at any time brought, but, being moved by *pneuma hagiôn*, men spake from‖ God."

---

* The words "in your hearts" must be read with "taking heed" for this is where the heed is to be taken. It cannot mean that the ungodly are to take heed to the prophetic word until they are converted; but that the children of God are to give heart-heed to prophecy until its consummation takes place in the rising of the Morning Star, and the dawning of that future Day for which we wait.

Modern teachers tell us that prophecy is a dark place, and we do well to avoid it; but this Scripture declares that this world is a dark place, and we do well to take heed to the prophetic word as being the only light that shines in it, and illumines us in the darkness.

† γίνομαι (ginomai) *to become, come to be, arise, originate, come into existence.*

‡ ἰδίας (idias) *its own.* ἰδίος (idios) occurs 113 times in the New Testament, and is never rendered "private" elsewhere. This is very significant: it at once arrests our attention, and points us to the true solution of the difficulty. 77 times it is rendered *own*: e.g., *his own* people, *his own* servants, *his own* sheep, *his own* country, &c., &c. The other places are similarly rendered. We may well therefore make this a 78th rendering and translate it *its own.*

§ ἐπίλυσις (epilusis) *a loosening upon.* As this word occurs nowhere else, its meaning must be determined

(1) by its *etymology*
(2) by its *usage*, and
(3) by the *scope* of passage.

(1) Its etymology is ἐπί (epi) *upon*, and λύω (luō) *to loosen.* Greek writers use it only two or three times, of *loosening the*

The notes below show us very clearly that the scope of the whole passage is the origin of the prophetic word.

1. It never came from its own sending forth, because

2. It never at any time came by the will of man, and therefore not from the prophets' own inner consciousness.

3. The question then arises, How did the prophecy of the Scriptures come? And the answer is, "*from God.*" The prophets spake from Him, being borne along by *pneuma hagion*, or Divine " power from on high."

The word " God " being emphatic here, points us to the fact that He Himself is the alone source of Holy Scripture. " All Scripture is God-breathed " (2 Tim. iii. 16), and it is God, who " spake by the prophets."

He spake " by the mouth " of His holy prophets. The " mouth " and the *pen* were theirs, but the *words* were His.

As the trees are swayed and borne along* by the wind that sweeps by, and give forth each their peculiar sound, by which they can be distinguished by the practiced ear, even in the dark ; so, the prophets were borne along and swayed by the Divine breath, *pneuma hagion*, or " power from on high."

---

leash of dogs, and sending them forth on the earth. Also unfolding so as *to set loose* and expose what is folded up.

2. As to its *usage*, the word does not occur elsewhere in the whole Bible. Even the verb occurs only in Gen. xli. 12. Mark iv. 34, and Acts xix. 39. Where its meaning is seen to be *to make known, unfold* or *disclose.*

3. The scope of 2 Pet. i. 19-21, is certainly not interpretation. The passage does not speak of what Scripture *means*, but whence it " came." It refers not to the *sense* of Scripture, but its source ; not to its *interpretation*, but to its origin.

‖ All the critical Greek Texts and R.V. read ἀπό (*apo*) *from*, instead of οἱ ἅγιοι (*hoi hagioi*) *holy.*

* φερόμενοι (*pheromenoi*) *borne* or *carried* along.

They "spake from God." And, while the prophetic word was God's, the mouth, the voice, the caligraphy were peculiar to the individuals who came, like the trees, under the power of that heavenly wind.*

Both Versions insert the articles, and use Capital letters. The R.V. margin omits the article and says " Or, Holy Spirit."

1 JOHN

1 John 3:24 "We know that He abideth in us by *the pneuma* which He hath given us."

Here, notwithstanding the article, it is expressly stated to be what is "given us." It is not the Giver therefore, but the New nature which is the greatest of His gifts, by which we know that God abideth in us. This is why the New nature is called "spirit of God" (or Divine spirit) Rom. viii. 9.

The A.V. of 1611 had " s "; but current Editions of A.V. and the R.V. have " S."

1 John 4:1 (twice). " Beloved, believe not every *pneuma*, but try the *pneumata* whether they are of God."

There can be no doubt as to the usage here.

Spirits are of various kinds—They may be teaching " demons " or " deceiving angels " (1 Tim. iv. 1). All are called " spirits." Some are " more wicked " than others (Matt. xii. 45). There are spirits " different " from others (2 Cor. xi. 4). The Lord speaks of " this kind " (Matt. xvii. 21). It is sometimes difficult to distinguish them from good spirits from whom they differ. They deceive by transforming themselves and, like human ministers, appear to be " ministers of

---

* A newspaper recently described the performance of a great violinist, and, speaking of his interpretation of the composer's thoughts and intentions, said, " there was an effacement of self, but no effacement of individuality." This faintly describes the phenomena of inspiration.

righteousness," and "angels of light" (2 Cor. xi. 13—15). One of them so appeared, advertising the message and the meetings of Paul and Silas (Acts xvi. 16—18).

Our responsibility is, not to believe them, but to " try " them and test them.

How can this be done ? How are we to try them ? Only by the Word of God. We have no other test by which we may prove them.

By this we can try their teachings. By this we can try their doctrines. (Gal. i. 6—10). By this we can test their practices (1 Cor. xiv.). If many speak at the same time, we can at once test this by the Word, which says the speaking is to be " by course " (*i.e.* in succession) " one by one" (*v.* 31); and the reason is given, " For God is not the author of confusion " (*v.* 33). " The spirits of the prophets are subject to the prophets" (*v.* 32). If therefore we see that the speakers are under the 'control' of the spirits, and cannot speak or cannot be silent for some alleged reason, then it is clear that the spirits are not " subject " to the speakers, but that the speakers are subject to the spirits.

When are we to try the spirits if not now ? How are we to try them but by the Word of God ? No other test can take the place of this. We can be so easily misled by apparent results, or by our own tastes and feelings, that, if we use not this one and only judge we may be mistaken and deceived.

Both versions have " s " in each case.

1 John 4:2 (twice). " Hereby ye may get to know *the pneuma* of God : every *pneuma* that confesseth that Jesus Christ has come in the flesh is of God."

The A.V. of 1611 had " s " in both cases. Current Editions with R.V. have " S " in the first clause, and " s " in the second.

1 John 4:3   "And every *pneuma* that confesseth not that Jesus Christ has come in the flesh is not of God."

Both Versions have "S."

The contrast is between evil *pneumata* and *pneumata* from God.

And here we have one of the tests.   Not the only one: for in Gal. i., we have a test as to *doctrine*; in 1 Cor. xiv. we have several tests as to *order*.   Here we have a test as to the teaching concerning the person and coming of the Lord Jesus.

These may not always be the marks in every case. One class may stand one test but not the others, and *vice versa*.

It is important and interesting to note the exact tenses used with regard to this particular test.

In chap. iv. 2, 3, it is the *Perfect* tense ἐληλυθότα (*eteluthota*) *has come.*

In chap. v. 6, it is the *Aorist* or simple past: ὁ ἐλθών (*ho elthōn*) *he that came.*

In 2 John 7, it is the *Present,* ἐρχόμενον (*erchomenon*) *coming,* or, [*the*] *coming one.*

Deceiving spirits deny these facts concerning the person and coming of the Lord Jesus Christ.

1 John 4:6   (twice).   "Hereby we get to know the *pneuma* of truth, and the *pneuma* of error."

By the test of the Word of God we get to know a true *pneuma* who speaks the truth from God; and a deceiving *pneuma* who speaks lies.   This latter word " deceiving," is the same as in 1 Tim. iv. 1.   Where it is rendered "seducing; " which means deceiving by lies, and false representations.

Both Versions have " s."

1 John 4:13   Hereby we get to know that we abide

in Him, and He in us, because he hath given us of His *pneuma.*

Here the word " of " is the Greek ἐκ (*ek*) *out of, from ;* and the meaning is that He hath given us gifts from His Spirit : spiritual gifts, " power from on high."

Both Versions have Capital letters.

1 John 5:6-8 (four times). " It is *the pneuma* that beareth witness, because *the pneuma* is truth. (7) For there are three that bear record [. . . .] (8) *The pneuma* and the water, and the blood, and these three agree in one.

In all the Critical Greek Texts and R.V. the rest of verse 7 and the first part of verse 8 goes out. So that the *pneuma hagion* of verse 7 is the ninth and last place where *pneuma* is to be omitted.

The words are not found in any Greek Manuscript before Cent. xvi., nor in any ancient Version. They are never quoted by the Greek Fathers, even when writing in support of the doctrine of the Trinity ; and they are not included in any of the Critical Greek Texts. They are first found in the Complutensian Polyglot of Cardinal Ximines (1514). Erasmus asked the Editors whether there were any Greek MSS. with these words. One of the Editors replied that the Greek MSS. were corrupt, and the Latin MSS. were true. Erasmus however, unfortunately pledged himself to include it in his Greek Text if *one* could be found. One was found, a Greek Codex, called by Erasmus a " Codex Britannicus." It is known as Codex Montfortianus (because it formerly belonged to Dr. Montfort of Cambridge) and is now in the Library of Trinity College, Dublin.

Erasmus kept his promise, and inserted the passage in the *third* edition of his Greek Testament, 1522.

It seems therefore that the passage was never in any

Greek MSS. before Cent. xvi.; that it was first seen in the margin of some Latin copies, in Africa; that from them it crept into the Text of two or three later Greek codices; and thence into the printed Greek Text, to which it never had any claim.

JUDE

Jude 19 " These are they who separate themselves, natural men,* not having *pneuma*": *i.e.*, not having the New nature, which is the gift of the Holy Spirit. The A.V. of 1611 had a small " s " here; but, current Editions with R.V., have a capital " S."

Jude 20 " Praying with (or by) *pneuma hagion* " *i.e.*, praying with " power from on high."

Both Versions insert the Article, and use Capital letters.

REVELATION

Rev. 1:4 " *The* seven *pneumata* which are before the throne."

This also had a small " s " in the A.V. of 1611, and so it should have been kept. The Current Editions of A.V., with R.V., have " S."

When we are distinctly told that there is only " one Spirit " (Eph. iv. 4), how can we understand this number, " seven," or any other, as being used of the Holy Spirit?

The Apocalypse is full of references to the doings of these same " seven angels "; who, as the " servants " of God find their proper place " before " the throne.

But, surely, if the Holy Spirit be God, he must be *on* the throne.

---

* ψυχικοί (*psychikoi*) *natural, soulical;* men, as being merely " *living souls.*" *See* 1 Cor. xv. 44. Compare 1 Cor. ii. 14.

It is assumed that the Trinity is mentioned or referred to in these verses (4 and 5) ; but it is only an assumption. There is no reason whatever why we should create such a difficulty for ourselves.

The *theme* of the book is judgment. Its *scope* is "the Day of the Lord." And, in those judgment scenes, special angels are mentioned as being assessors, holding high office and estate—as principalities and powers. See Matt. xvi. 27. "The Son of Man shall come in the glory of His Father with His angels." See 1 Tim. v. 21. "I charge thee before the Lord Jesus Christ and the elect angels." (Compare Acts viii. 29.)

The Article denotes the "seven angels" referred to throughout the Apocalypse.

Those who take this as referring to the Holy Spirit Himself refer to Is. xi. 2. But there is no number mentioned there. Seven spiritual gifts are enumerated, and designated ; but this is quite a different thing, and affords no warrant for such a polytheistic interpretation. (*See* Matt. xii. 18).

Rev. 1:10 "I became by [the] *pneuma* in the Lord's day." The A.V. of 1611 had a "s." Current Editions with R.V. have "S." The article is latent after the preposition *ἐν (en) by* ; and, what we are told is that, John, by* the power and agency of the Holy Spirit was transported into a sphere of heavenly vision, where he saw the future scenes of judgment unveiled, which will one day be a dread reality.

What that power was may be seen from analogous cases.

---

* *See* Matt. ix. 34. "He casteth out devils *through* the prince of the devils." Matt. v. 34, 35. "Swear not at all, neither *by* heaven, nor *by* the earth, for it is His footstool. So *ἐν (en)* is often rendered. *See* Lu. xxii. 49. Heb. xi. 37. Rev. ii. 16 ; vi. 8 ; xiii. 10 (" Slain *by* or *with* the sword.")

Ezekiel saw visions of future glory "by the Spirit." Ezek. xi. 24, 25 ; xl. 2, 3. Compare Ezek. i. 1, and viii. 3, where "the form of an hand" was put forth, and Ezekiel was lifted up between the earth and the heaven. *See* also Acts viii. 39.

Rev. 2:7,11,17,29   In all these places we have the article, referring to the Holy Spirit.

These seven Epistles differ from the Epistles to the seven Pauline Churches (Rom. Cor. Gal. Eph. Phil. Col. Thess.), in that they are addressed by Christ, through John : while the others are addressed by the Holy Spirit through Paul.

In both cases the Spirit is the medium of the inspired record.

They are alike in number, but that is all.

They are addressed in the *present* tense, by Christ, who is absent from them ; the Spirit also is absent, as was the Apostle John.

The official absence of the Spirit shows that there had been a change in the dispensation.

Paul's Epistles, on the other hand, came from the Father and the Son as absent in Heaven ; but not from the Spirit, because He was present on earth, and in communion or fellowship with the saints (2 Cor. xiii. 14).

Hence, the conclusion is that, when the days shall have come which are referred to in Rev. ii. and iii., the Church of God will have been caught up to meet the Lord in the air ; the Holy Spirit will likewise have gone ; and the assemblies there addressed are assemblies in a Dispensation of judgment, and not in this Dispensation of grace.

The characteristics of the Dispensations are thus marked.

1.   In the Dispensation of Law, Jehovah was regarded

as specially present. The Shekinah between the Cherubim was the symbol of His presence.

Christ was "the coming one," not yet Incarnate. And the Spirit "came upon" individuals from time to time, endowing them with different "powers" for service.

2. The Dispensation of "the coming One" ("the days of the Son of Man"), was characterised by the presence and manifestation of Christ on earth, proclaiming Himself as King, and His kingdom as being "at hand." The Spirit was absent in Heaven, acting "upon" individuals on earth.

3. The present Dispensation of Grace, is characterised by the absence of Christ on account of His rejection; and the presence of the Holy Spirit in fulfilment of the promise of the Father.

4. The Dispensation of Judgment will be characterised by the absence of the Spirit, and the speedily coming presence of Christ, who will then be about to execute judgment in the earth.

The Epistles to the seven assemblies of Rev. ii., iii., are to be interpreted therefore of that special period, after the Spirit shall have left the earth with the Church of God, and immediately before the Advent of Christ in judgment.*

Rev. 3:1 "*The* seven *pneumata* of God." The same as in ch. i. 4.

Both Versions have " S."

Rev. 3:6,13,22 The same as in ch. ii. 7. *See* above.

Rev. 4:2 The same as ch. i. 10.

Rev. 4:5 The same as ch. i. 4.

---

* See *Things to Come* for October, 1903. Vol. x., page 44.

Rev. 5:6   The same as ch. i. 4.

Rev. 11:11   " After three days and a half a *pneuma* of life from God entered into them, and they stood upon their feet."

Here *pneuma* is psychological, according to Gen. ii. 7. It is the Genitive of origin or source.   A *pneuma* that gave life and made the bodies become " living souls."

The A.V. has " S."   The R.V. translates it " breath.'

Rev. 13:15   He (the 2nd Beast) had power to give *pneuma* unto the image of the Beast."

This could not be the Holy Spirit.   The A.V. renders it " life " and puts " Greek, *breath* " in the margin.   The R.V. puts " breath " in the text, and nothing in the margin.

But there is no need thus to vary the translation if we keep to the psychological use of *pneuma*.

Rev. 14:13   "Yea, saith *the pneuma*."   Here the article and the context denote the Holy Spirit.

Rev. 16:13   " Three unclean *pneumata*."   These are explained in the next verse as being

Rev. 16:14   "*Pneumata* of demons."   Here it is the Genitive of apposition.   " They are *pneumata*, that is to say, demons " or simply " *pneumata* which are demons."

Demons have not " spirits," as human beings have ; they *are* spirits, or spirit-beings.   There is no article in the Greek, in either verse.

Both Versions have " s " in both verses (*vv*. 13, 14).

Rev. 17:3   *See* ch. i. 10.   Both Versions have " S."

Rev. 18:2   " Babylon is become the hold of every foul *pneuma*," *i.e.*, of every unclean spirit.

Both Versions have " s."

Rev. 19:10   " The testimony of Jesus is *the pneuma* of prophecy.

The first question is, How are these two Genitives to be taken ?   Is " the testimony of Jesus," His testimony which He gave ? Or, our testimony concerning Him which we give ? In other words, Is it the Gen. of possession, or relation ?

In either case it is the very essence of all prophecy. For *pneuma* here, must be taken in the sense of usage No. vii., denoting essence or character.

Both Versions have " s."

Rev. 21:10   " And he carried me away in *pneuma* :" *i.e.*, by [the] *pneuma*. *See* under ch. i. 10.

Rev. 22:6   This is the third of the three places* where *pneumata* is to be added, according to all the Critical Greek Texts, and the R.V.

According to these the words πνευμάτων τῶν (*pneumatōn tōn*) *of the spirits of the*, are to be substituted for the word ἁγίων (*hagiōn*) *holy*.

So that instead of reading as the A.V. " the Lord God of the holy Prophets sent his angel," we should read— " And the Lord, the God of the *pneumata* of the prophets, sent His angel.

Here *pneumata* would denote the spiritual gifts of the prophets. He, and He alone, is the giver of their gifts. He it was " who spake by the prophets," and they owe their gift of prophecy to the same One who gave them life.

Rev. 22:17   " The Spirit and the bride say Come." Here, it is the Holy Spirit, and it is to be interpreted by chap. ii. 7, of the time when Paradise will be restored; and man, no longer driven forth, will be invited back to

---

* The other two being Acts iv. 25, and Phil. iv. 23.

it. It will be the mission of the Holy Spirit then, and the Bride, to invite the long-exiled nations of mankind to again enjoy the beauties and glories of a restored creation, to eat of the tree of life, and to drink of the water of life in the midst of the Paradise of God.

APPENDIX 1

Classified List of Usages of *Pneuma*

* is *pneuma hagion*.

** is *hagion pneuma*.

( ) denotes a passage in which the word *pneuma* is to be omitted or added.

† denotes a various reading affecting the passage as well as the word *pneuma*.

I.—GOD. John iv. 24 (first). 1 Cor. iii. 16.

II.—CHRIST. 1 Cor. vi. 17. 2 Cor. iii. 17 (twice), 18.

III.—THE HOLY SPIRIT. Matt. i. 20; iii. 16†; iv. 1; x. 20; xii. 28, 31, 32; xxii. 43; xxviii. 19. Mark i. 10, 12; iii. 29; xii. 36; xiii. 11. Luke ii. 26, 27; iv. 1 (second), 14; x. 21†; xii. 10. John i. 32, 33 (first); iii. 6 (first), 8 (twice), 34†; xiv. 17, 26; xv. 26; xvi. 13. Acts i. 16; ii. 4 (second); v. 3, 9; vii. 51; ix. 31**; xi. 28; xiii. 2, 4; xv. 28; xvi. 6, 7†; xx. 23, 28; xxi. 4; xxviii. 25. Rom. viii. 16 (first), 26 (twice), 27; xv. 16, 30. 1 Cor. ii. 10 (twice)†, 11 (second), 14; vi. 11; vii. 8; xii. 4, 7, 8 (twice), 11. 2 Cor. xiii. 14**. Gal. iii. 14; v. 22; vi. 8 (second). Eph. i. 13; ii. 18; iii. 5, 16; iv. 3, 4, 30; (v. 9† omit); v. 18; vi. 17, 18. 2 Thess. ii. 13. 1 Tim. iv. 1 (first). Heb. iii. 7; ix. 8, 14; x. 15, 29. 1 Pet. i. 2, 11 (22 omit); iv. 14. 1 John iv. 2 (first); v. 6 (twice), (7 omit)†, 8. Rev. i. 10; ii. 7, 11, 17, 29; iii. 6, 13, 22; iv. 2; xiv. 13; xvii. 3; xxi. 10; xxii. 17.

IV.—THE OPERATIONS OF THE HOLY SPIRIT.

(*) Passages marked thus are *pneuma hagion*: repeated again, separately, in Usage No. xiv. below.

Matt. i. 18*; iii. 11*; xii. 18. Mark i. 8*. Luke i. 15*, 17, 35*, 41*, 67*; ii. 25*; iii. 16*; iv. 1* (first), 18; xi. 13*. John i. 33* (second); iii. 5, 6 (second); iv. 23, 24 (second); vii. 39 (twice); xx. 22*. Acts 1, 2*, 5* 8*; ii. 4* (first), 17, 18, 33**; iv. 8* (25* add), 31*; v. 32†; vi. 3 (*), 5*, 10; vii. 55*; viii. 15*, 17*, 18*†, 19*; ix. 17*; x. 38*, 44, 45**, 47; xi. 15, 16*, 24*; xiii. 9*, 52*; xv. 8; xix. 2* (twice)† 6*.

Rom. v. 5* ; ix. 1* ; xiv. 17* ; xv. 13, 19. 1 Cor. ii. 4†, 13† ;
vi. 19** ; vii. 40 ; xii. 3* (second), 13 (twice)† ; xiv. 2, 12.
2 Cor i. 22 ; iii. 3 ; iv. 13 ; v. 5 ; vi. 6*. Gal. v. 5. Eph. i.
13, 17. 1 Thess. i. 5*, 6* ; iv. 8† ; v, 19. 2 Tim. i. 14*† ;
Titus iii. 5*. Heb. ii. 4* ; vi. 4*. 1 Pet. i. 12*. 2 Pet. i. 20*.
1 John iii. 24 ; iv. 13. Jude 20* (Rev. xxii. 6 add).

V.—THE NEW NATURE. Rom. viii. (1 omit)†, 2, 4, 5 (twice),
6, 9 (three times), 10, 11 (twice)†, 13, 14, 16 (second), 23.
1 Cor. ii. 12 (second) ; xii. 3 (first), 14 ; xiv. 15 (twice), 16,
32. Gal. iii. 2, 3, 5 ; iv. 6, 29 ; v. 16, 17 (twice), 18, 25
(twice); vi. 8 (first). Eph. iv. 23. 1 John iii. 24. Jude 19.

VI.—PSYCHOLOGICAL. Matt. xxvii. 50. Mark xv. 39. Luke
i. 80 ; (ii. 40 omit) ; viii. 55 ; xxiii. 46. John vi. 63 (twice),
xix. 30. Acts vii. 59. 1 Cor. ii. 11 (first), 12 (first) ; v. 5 ;
(vi. 20 omit) ; vii. 34†. 2 Cor. iii. 6 (twice). 1 Thess. v. 23.
Heb. iv. 12 ; xii, 23. Jas. ii. 26 ; iv. 5. Rev. xi. 11 ; xiii. 15.

VII.—CHARACTER. Matt. v. 3. (Luke ix. 5† omit). Rom.
viii. 15 (twice). 1 Cor. iv. 21. Gal. vi. 1. (1 Tim. iv. 12
omit). 2 Tim. i. 7. 1 Pet. iii. 4. Rev. xix. 10.

VIII.—METONYMY (put for that which is invisible as opposed to
the flesh : *e.g.*, *will*, *mind*, &c., or that which is supernatural :
spiritual supplies (marked s) ; supernatural judgment (marked
j).
Matt. xxvi. 41. Mark xiv. 38. Acts xvii. 16 ; (xviii. 5
omit)†. 1 Cor. v. 4. 2 Cor. xii. 18. Phil. i. 27s ; ii. i.
2 Thess. ii. 8j.

IX.—SYNECDOCHE (a part put for the whole ; *e.g.*, *pneuma* put
for one's self).
Mark ii. 8 ; viii. 12. Luke i. 47. John xi. 33 ; xiii. 21.
1 Cor. xiv. 14 ; xvi. 18. 2 Cor. ii. 13 ; vii. 1, 13. Gal. vi. 18.
(Phil. iv. 23 add). 2 Tim. iv. 22†. Philem. 25.

X.—ADVERBIAL (implying *essence* ; or whatever is spoken of as
possessed or done, as being so in the highest degree).

Acts xviii. 25 ; xix. 21 ; xx. 22. Rom. i. 9 ; ii. 29 ; vii. 6 ;
xii. 11. 1 Cor. v. 3. Phil. iii. 3†. Col. i. 8 ; ii. 5.

XI.—ANGELS or spirit-beings. (Neutral marked n).
Luke xxiv. 37, 39. Acts viii. 29, 39 ; x. 19 ; xi. 12 ; xxiii. 8n,
9n. Heb. i. 7, 14 ; xii. 9n. 1 Pet. iii. 19. 1 John iv. 2n
(second), 6 (first). Rev. i. 4 ; iii. 1 ; iv. 5 ; v. 6.

XII.—DEMONS or evil-spirits. (n = neutral).
Matt. viii. 16; x. 1 ; xii. 43, 45. Mark i. 23, 26, 27 ; iii. 11,
30 ; v. 2, 8, 13 ; vi. 7 ; vii. 25 ; ix. 17, 20, 25 (twice). Luke
iv. 33, 36 ; vi. 18 ; vii. 21 ; viii. 2, 29 ; ix. 39, 42 ; x. 20 ; xi.

24, 26 ; xiii. 11.   Acts v. 16; viii. 7 ; xvi. 16, 18 ; xix. 12, 13, 15, 16 ; xxiii. 8n.   1 Cor. xii. 10n.   2 Cor. xi. 4n.   Eph. ii. 2 [vi. 12].   2 Thess ii. 2.   1 Tim. iv. 1 (second),   1 John iv. 1 (twice), 3, 6 (second).   Rev. xvi. 13, 14 ; xviii. 2.

XIII.—THE RESURRECTION BODY.   (" Flesh and bones ").
Rom. i. 4.   1 Cor. xv. 45.   1 Tim. iii. 16.   Heb. xii. 23. 1 Pet. iii. 18 ; iv. 6.

XIV.—PNEUMA HAGION (included in No. IV. above, *hagion pneuma* marked [h.p.]
Matt. i. 18 ; iii. 11.   Mark i. 8.   Luke i. 15, 35, 41, 67 ; ii. 25 ; iii. 16 ; iv. 1 (first) ; xi. 13.   John i. 33 (second) ; xx. 22. Acts i. 2, 5, 8 ; ii. 4 (first), 33, 38[h.p.] iv. 8 (25 add), 31 ; vi. 3†, 5 ; vii. 55 ; viii, 15, 17 (18†), 19 ; ix. 17 ; x. 38 ; xi. 16, 24 ; xiii. 9, 52 ; xix. 2 (twice), 6.   Rom. v. 5 ; ix. 1 ; xiv. 17. 1 Cor. ii. 13† ; vi. 19[h.p.] ; xii. 3 (second).   2 Cor. vi. 6. 1 Thess. i. 5, 6.   2 Tim. i. 14†.   Titus iii. 5.   Heb. ii. 4 ; vi. 4.   1 Pet. i. 12.   2 Pet. i. 20.   Jude 20.

APPENDIX 2

Classified List of References
in Which *Pneuma* Occurs

Pneuma is used of

1. GOD (John iv. 24. 1 Cor. iii. 16), as the source of life in all its manifestations.

2. CHRIST (1 Cor. vi. 17. 2 Cor. iii. 17, 18).

3. THE HOLY SPIRIT. Generally with the article; but not always, or necessarily so.

4. THE OPERATIONS OF THE HOLY SPIRIT. Spiritual gifts (1 Cor. xiv. 32). Passages marked with asterisk (*) are *pneuma hagion*. See No. 14 below.

5. THE NEW NATURE, as the greatest of His gifts. This is more especially the Pauline usage: *spirit* as opposed to flesh (John iii. 6. Rom. viii. 4, &c.).

6. MAN (Psychologically). Spirit as imparted to man, making him "a living soul" (Gen. ii. 7. Ps. civ. 29, 30. Ecc. xii. 7). When taken back to and by God, man becomes "a dead soul." The Heb. *Nephesh* (soul) is translated "body" in Lev. xxi. 11. Num. vi. 6; xix. 11, 13. "Dead body" Num. ix. 6, 7, 10. Hag. ii. 13. And, "the dead," Lev. xix. 28; xxi. 1; xxii. 4. Num. v. 2; vi. 11).

7. CHARACTER, as being in itself invisible and manifested only in one's actions (2 Tim. i. 7. Rom. viii. 15, &c.).

8. OTHER INVISIBLE CHARACTERISTICS (by *Metonymy*): such as *feelings* or *desires* (Matt. xxvi. 41, &c.): or for that which is supernatural, Spiritual *supplies* marked ("s"), and supernatural judgments marked "j."

9. THE WHOLE PERSON (by *Synecdoche*), a part being but for the whole (Luke i. 47).

10. ADVERBIALLY, either in Dative case, or with a Preposition, as ἐν δόλῳ, *craftily* (2 Cor. xi. 16), ἐν τάχει, *quickly* (Rev. i. 1), &c.

11.—ANGELS, or SPIRIT-BEINGS (Heb. i. 7, 14. Acts viii. 29.
Rev. i. 4, &c.) As to 1 Pet. iii. 19, the following should be
noted:—

πνεύματα, *spirits*, when standing alone (without any
qualifying words, as it does here), is never used of men in
any form, state or condition. These are spiritual beings.
He "maketh His angels spirits"(Heb. i. 7, 14. Ps. civ. 4).
The angels who sinned in Gen. vi. 2, 4, see 2 Pet. ii. 4-9 and
Jude 6, 7. The term "sons of God" (Gen. vi. 2, 4) is
always used of angels (see Job ii. 1 ; xxxviii. 7. Ps. xxix. 1 ;
lxxxix. 6. Dan. iii. 25 (Codex A of the lxx. in Gen. vi. 2
reads " ἄγγελοι τοῦ Θεοῦ, *angels of God*). They left their
own "habitation" (οἰκητήριον occurs only here and 2
Cor. v. 2, where it is used of a *spiritual body !*). For their
sin they were "cast down to Tartarus," delivered unto
chains of darkness " ; in other words, put " in prison " and
reserved unto the judgment of the great day. Christ's
triumph was so complete that the proclamation of it
reached even to Tartarus. In the structure of the passage,
verse 20 corresponds to verse-22 : in verse 20 we have the
disobedience of these spirits, while in verse -22 we have their
subjection. See page 188-193 above, also a pamphlet
by the same author and publisher, on *the Spirits in Prison*,
wherein this Scripture is expounded in the light of the
Epistle as a whole. The passage is introduced for the purpose of proving that " it is better, if the will of God be so,
that ye suffer for well doing than for evil doing, FOR Christ
also once suffered, &c." The argument and scope being :
' He had a glorious triumph (Eph. iv. 8. Col. ii. 15. 1 Pet.
i. 21) ; so will you in like manner. Even when angels were
put in prison, men (Noah and Lot) were delivered. You
will likewise be delivered from your tribulation.'
Neutral or doubtful usages marked " n."

12. DEMONS or EVIL SPIRIT-BEINGS (doubtful or neutral, marked
" n.")

13. THE RESURRECTION BODY (1 Cor. xv. 45 ; 1 Pet. iii. 18 ; and
iv. 6. As to the last passage we may note that in
the A.V. and R.V. the particle μέν, *though*, is left untranslated. It does not say that the Gospel was preached to
them "that they might be judged," but, that "*though*
(μέν) they might be judged." They might be judged
indeed (μέν) by man's tribunal (κατὰ ἀνθρώπους, *according
to* the will of *men*, see Rom. viii. 27 ; xv. 5. I Cor. xii. 8 ;
xv. 32. 2 Cor. vii. 9, 10, 11 ; xi. 17. Gal. i. 11. Eph. ii. 2.
Col. ii. 8 ; 1 Peter iv. 14). They might be put to death indeed (μέν) as regards the flesh (σαρκί, the Dat. of reference), yet (δὲ) they shall live according to the will of God

(κατά θεόν, see the refs. above). For this cause—to give them this hope—was the Gospel preached to them as is described in 1 Pet. i, 12, 25. The hope of glory was set over against their sufferings (see 1 Pet. i. 11 ; iv. 13).

In Heb. xii. 23 just men will not be "perfected" till their spirits are (returned to God) united to the risen body in resurrection.

14. PNEUMA HAGION. This expression (which occurs fifty times) without articles, is never used of the GIVER (the Holy Spirit), but always of His GIFT. What this gift is may be seen by comparing Acts. i. 4, 5 with Luke xxiv. 49, where "the promise of the Father" is (in Acts) called *pneuma hagion* (holy spirit), and (in Luke) it is called "power from on high." This "power" includes whatever spiritual gifts the Holy Spirit may be pleased to bestow.

This will be found the case in every one of the fifty occurrences. In Acts ii. 4 we read "they were all filled with *pneuma hagion*, and began to speak with other tongues as THE SPIRIT gave :" *pneuma hagion* is here, and always, *what is given*, not the Giver.

Pneuma hagion is usually translated "the Holy Spirit," the article being inserted, and capital letters used. But then we have no stronger expression by which to translate "*to pneuma, to hagion*" (the Spirit, the holy [Spirit]).

We must be careful to distinguish that which is so clearly marked in the Original.

Whenever spirit is said to *fall*, or to be *given*, or to *fill*, or be *baptized with*, it is always *pneuma* without the article, or *pneuma hagion*.

4*	Matt. i.	18, 20		12.	Mark i.	23, 26, 27.
4*	,,	iii. 11		9.	,,	ii. 8
3.	,,	16		12.	,,	iii. 11
3.	,,	iv. 1		3.	,,	29
7.	,,	v. 3		12,	,,	30
12.	,,	vii. 16		12.	,,	v. 2, 8, 13
12.	,,	x. 1		12.	,,	vi. 7
8.	,,	20		—.	,,	49 (The word is
4.	,,	xii. 18			φάντασμα, *a phantom*).	
3.	,,	28, 31, 32		12.	,,	vii. 25
12.	,,	43, 45		9.	,,	viii. 12
—.	,,	xiv. 26 (The word is		12.	,,	ix. 17, 20, 25 (twice)
	φάντισμα, *a phantom*).			3.	,,	xii. 36
3.	,,	xxii. 43		3.	,,	xiii. 11
8.	,,	xxvi. 41		8.	,,	xiv. 38
6.	,,	xxvii. 50		6.	,,	xv. 39
3.	,,	xxviii. 19		4*	Luke i.	15
4*	Mark i.	8		4.	,,	17
3.	,,	10, 12		4*	,,	35, 41

9.	Luke	i.	47
4*	,,		67
6.	,,		80
4*	,,	ii.	25
3.	,,		26, 27
6.	,,		40 (omit All)
4*	,,	iii.	16
4*	,,	iv.	1 (first)
3.	,,		1 (second), 14
4.	,,		18
12.	,,		33, 36
12.	,,	vi.	18
12.	,,	vii.	21
12.	,,	viii.	2, 29
6	,,		55
12.	,,	ix.	39, 42
7.	,,		55
12.	,,	x.	20
3.	,,		21 (add ἐν, by, and τῷ ἁγίῳ, the holy).
12.			24, 26
4*	,,	xi.	13
3.	,,	xii.	10
12.	,,	xiii.	11
6.	,,	xxiii.	46
11.	,,	xxiv.	37, 39
3.	John	i.	32, 33 (first)
4*	,,		33 (second)
4.	,,	iii.	5
3.	,,		6 (first)
4.	,,		6 (second)
3.	,,		8 (twice), 34 (om. ὁ θεὸς, L.Trb. T.A.WH. and R.V.).
4.	,,	iv.	23
1.	,,		24 (first)
4.	,,		24 (second)
6.	,,	vi	63 (twice)
4.	,,	vii.	39 (twice)
9.	,,	xi.	33
9.	,,	xiii.	21
3.	,,	xiv.	17, 26
3.	,,	xv.	26
3.	,,	xvi.	13
6.	,,	xix.	30
4*	,,	xx.	22
4*	Acts	i.	2, 5, 8
3.	,,		16
4*	,,	ii.	4 (first)

3.	Acts	ii.	4 (second)
4.	,,		17, 18
4**	,,		33
4*	,,	iv.	8
4*	,,		25 (add All) 31
3.	,,	v.	3, 9
12.	,,		16
4.	,,		32†
4*	,,	vi.	3, 5, 10
3.	,,	vii.	51
4*	,,		55
6.	,,		59
12.	,,	viii.	7
4*	,,		15, 17, 18 (om. τὸ ἅγιον, L.T.Trb. A. and R.V.) 19.
11.			29, 39
4*	,,	ix.	17
3**	,,		31
11.	,,	x.	19
4*	,,		38
4.	,,		44
4**	,,		45
4.	,,		47
11.	,,		19
4*	,,		38
4.	,,		44
4**	,,		45
4.	,,		47
11.	,,	xi.	12
4.	,,		15
4*	,,		16, 24
3.	,,		28
3.	,,	xiii.	2, 4
4*	,,		9, 52
4.	,,	xv.	8
3.	,,		28
3.	,,	xvi.	6, 7 (add Ἰησοῦ Jesus, All and R.V.)
12.	,,		16, 18
8.	,,	xvii.	16
8.	,,	xviii.	5 (λόγῳ, engrossed in the word. All)
10.	,,	xviii.	25
4*	,,	xix.	2 (twice), 6
12.	,,		12, 13, 15, 16
10.	,,		21
10.	,,	xx.	22

11or12.	Acts	xxiii.	8, 9
3.	,,	xxviii.	25
13.	Rom.	i.	4
10.	,,		9
10.	,,	ii.	29
4*	,,	v.	5
10.	,,	vii.	6
5.	,,	viii.	1 (*om*. All), 2, 4, 5 (twice),6, 9 (three times),10,11 (twice) 13, 14.
7.	,,		15 (twice)
3.	,,		16 (first)
5.	,,		16 (second), 23
3.	,,		26 (twice), 27
4*	,,	ix.	1
10.	,,	xii.	11
4*	,,	xiv.	17
4.	,,	xv.	13
3.	,,		16
4.	,,		19
1.	,,		30
4.	1 Cor.	ii.	4
6.	,,		11 (first)
3.	,,		11 (second)
6.	,,		12 (first)
5.	,,		12 (second)
4.	,,		13 (*om*. ἅγιον, *holy*, All.)
3.	,,		14
1.	,,	iii.	16
7.	,,	iv.	21
10.	,,	v.	3
8.	,,		4
6.	,,		5
3.	,,	vi.	11
2.	,,		17
4**	,,		19
6.	,,		20 (*om*. All).
3.	,,	vii.	8
6.	,,		34 (*add* Art., All).
4.	,,		40
5.	,,	xii.	3 (first).
4*	,,		3 (second).
3.	,,		4, 7, 8 (twice).
12.	,,		10
3.	,,		11
4.	,,		13 (twice).
4.	,,	xiv.	2, 12
9.	1 Cor.	xiv.	14
13.	,,	xv.	45
9.	,,	xvi.	18
4.	2 Cor.	i.	22
9.	,,	ii.	13
4.	,,	iii.	3
6.	,,		6 (twice), 8
2.	,,		17 (twice), 18
4.	,,	iv.	13
4.	,,	v.	5
4*	,,	vi.	6
9.	,,	vii.	1, 13
12.	,,	xi.	4_n
8.	,,	xii.	18
3**	,,	xiii.	14
5.	Gal.	iii.	2, 3, 5
3.	,,		14
5.	,,	iv.	6, 29
4.	,,	v.	5
5.	,,		16, 17 (twice), 18
3.	,,		22
5.	,,		25 (twice).
7.	,,	vi.	1
5.	,,		8 (first).
3.	,,		8 (second).
9.	,,		18
3 or 4	Eph.	i.	13
4.	,,		17
12.	,,	ii.	2
3.	,,	iii.	5, 16
3.	,,	iv.	3, 4
5.	,,		23
3.	,,		30
3.	,,	v.	9 (φωτός, *of light*. All).
3.	,,		18
3.	,,	vi.	17, 18
8.	Phil.	i.	27
8.	,,	ii.	1
10.	,,	iii.	3
9.	,,	iv.	(23 *add* instead of "A on all," All).
10.	Col.	i.	8
10.	,,	ii.	5
4*	1 Thess.	i.	5, 6
4.	,,	iv.	8
4.	,,	v.	10
6.	,,		23
12.	2 Thess.	ii.	2
8.	,,		8

3.	2 Thess.	ii.	**13**
13.	1 Tim.	iii.	**16**
3.	,,	iv.	**1** (first)
12.	,,		**1** (second)
7.	,,		**12** (*omit*, All).
7.	2 Tim.	i.	**7**
4*	,,		**14**
9.	,,	iv.	**22**
4*	Titus	iii.	**5**
9.	Philem.		**25**
4*	Heb.	ii.	**4**
3.	,,	iii.	**7**
6.	,,	iv.	**12**
4*	,,	vi.	**4**
3.	,,	ix.	**8, 14**
3.	,,	x.	**15, 29**
6 and 12.		xii.	**23** (see above, under No. 12, page 210).
6.	James	ii.	**26**
6.	,,	iv.	**5**
3.	1 Peter	i.	**2, 11**
4.	,,		**12**
3.	,,		**22** (*omit*, All).
13.	,,	iii.	**18** (see page 188)
13.	,,	iv.	**6** (see page193)
4*	2 Peter	i.	**20**
4&5.	1 John	iii.	**24**
12.	,,	iv.	**1** (twice).

3.	1 John	iv.	**2**
12.	,,		**3**
11.	,,		**6** (first).
12.	,,		**6** (second).
4.	,,		**13**
3.	,,	v.	**6** (twice) **7, 8**
5.	Jude		**19**
4*	,,		**20**
11.	Rev.	i.	**4**
3.	,,		**10**
3.	,,	ii.	**7, 11, 17, 29**
11.	,,	iii.	**1**
3.	,,		**6, 13, 22**
3.	,,	iv.	**2**
11.	,,		**5**
11.	,,	v.	**6**
6.	,,	xi.	**11**
6.	,,	xiii.	**15**
3.	,,	xiv.	**13**
12.	,,	xvi.	**13, 14**
3.	,,	xvii.	**3**
12.	,,	xviii.	**2**
7.	,,	xix.	**10**
3,	,,	xxi.	**10**
4*	,,	xxii.	**6** (*add* πνευμάτων τῶν, *spirits of the*, All).
3.	,,		**17**

Index of Subjects

Index of Texts Explained

Index of Greek Words Explained

discipline

delight
in (the)
Spirit. celibrate
inwardly.

$9.99